# Protecting Your ASC
## A Legal Handbook

Federated Ambulatory Surgery Association
Alexandria, VA

# Editorial Staff

**Editor**
Kathy Bryant, Executive Director
*FASA*

**Authors**
Scott Becker
Scott Downing
Morgan Moran
*Ross & Hardies*

Copyright © 2002 by the Federated Ambulatory Surgery Association
All rights reserved. No part of this book may be reproduced or
transmitted in any form or by any means, electronic or mechanical,
including photocopying, recording or by an information storage and
retrieval system, without permission in writing from the publisher.

Federated Ambulatory Surgery Association
700 N. Fairfax St., #306
Alexandria, VA 22314-2040

ISBN 0-9719088-0-X
Printed in the United States of America

# Table of Contents

Acknowledgments ........................................................................iv

Introduction by Bob Williams ......................................................v

About the Authors ....................................................................vii


Chapter 1   Licensing and Certificate of Need Issues ...................1

Chapter 2   Medicare Certification.............................................11

Chapter 3   Governance ...............................................................15

Chapter 4   Compliance Plans .....................................................19

Chapter 5   Medical Staff Credentialing and Privileging ............31

Chapter 6   Employment Law Issues .........................................37

Chapter 7   Reporting Adverse Events ........................................49

Chapter 8   Taxation and Pension Planning Issues .....................51

Chapter 9   ASC Sales and Acquisitions......................................61

Chapter 10  Antitrust Considerations .........................................71

Chapter 11  Anti-Kickback and Self-Referral Laws ....................77

Chapter 12  False Claims Act ......................................................91


Appendix A  State Certificate of Need Laws ...............................96

Appendix B  Medicare ASC Regulations ....................................97

Endnotes ................................................................................112

Index .....................................................................................114

**Protecting Your ASC: A Legal Handbook**

# Acknowledgments

Undertaking a publication covering the diverse issues affecting ASCs today was an overwhelming task. Without the numerous people who contributed their time and unique expertise to this project, FASA could not have published this book. FASA is indebted to these individuals. A sincere thanks goes to the following individuals who served as continuing advisers from the first draft to the final copy. This group reviewed many drafts, identified omissions, raised concerns and perhaps most importantly helped with the transition from "legalese" to English. Without their insight and critical review, this book would not be available today.

- Lavern Bird, Director of Regional Operations, Johnson and Johnson Health Care Systems, Dubuque, IA
- Beth Derby, Executive Vice President, Health Resources International, LLC, West Hartford, CT
- Jerry Henderson, Executive Director, Surgicenter of Baltimore, Baltimore, MD
- Peter Lohrengel, Executive Director, Florida Society of ASCs, Tallahassee, FL
- Tom Wilson, Chief Executive Officer, Monterey Peninsula Surgery Center, Monterey, CA

Prior to her departure from FASA, Teresa Mayfield spent numerous hours working to bring this book to publication from design to editing. Her contribution is appreciated.

FASA would also like to thank Carol Beeler of Johnson and Johnson Health Care Systems, Inc., Cincinnati, OH; Nap Gary of HealthSouth, Birmingham, AL; Ron Moore of Surgex, Inc., Fort Worth, TX; Robin Stombler of the American Society of Clinical Pathologists, Washington, DC; and Jill Watson of Public Relations Rx, Kansas City, MO; for their contributions to this text.

# Introduction

The Federated Ambulatory Surgery Association (FASA) is pleased to publish this guide to the laws and regulations governing the ambulatory surgery industry. I think you will find this document an invaluable tool whether you are a newcomer to the industry or have been in the industry for years. While there are numerous publications available on the legal issues affecting health care facilities, relatively few address the issues facing the ambulatory surgery center (ASC) administrator and the owner. The laws and regulations governing ASCs are often different or apply differently to ASCs. Moreover, the legal publications tend to be written in "legalese," making use by those of us not trained in the law more time consuming than necessary. This publication is specifically written for the ASC administrator, with legal issues discussed in plain English for easy comprehension.

Every facet of the ASC business is governed by a variety of laws and regulations, from the planning stage, where some states require that a certificate of need (CON) be obtained to build an ASC, to the daily operations, to the point that some states govern how you dispose of medical records. This book covers issues relevant to those considering building an ASC, such as chapter 11's discussion of how financial investments must be structured; to those operating an ASC, such as chapter 6's discussion of employment laws; and even to those considering selling their ASC, such as chapter 9's discussion of sales and acquisitions. The appendixes provide the actual Medicare regulations and a list of states with certificate of need laws.

This handbook is intended to provide practical advice and an overview of many legal issues that ASCs regularly face. However, I must caution you that this book is not intended to be a substitute for your legal counsel.

**Protecting Your ASC: A Legal Handbook**

One publication could not possibly cover all the provisions of the laws and regulations in sufficient detail. Although this publication focuses on federal laws, we have tried to alert you to state law issues and in some cases discuss the laws of particular states as examples of state law. But this handbook does not provide an extensive discussion of state law. You definitely need to consult an attorney or a state-specific information source for those items.

This book should provide you a useful framework and general understanding of many of the legal issues that ASCs face. This improved understanding of these issues should help you deal with such issues on a day-to-day basis and should enhance your ability to work in an efficient manner with your ASC's legal counsel. I wish this book would have been available to me when I began in this industry more than two decades ago.

Bob Williams
President, 2000–2002
Federated Ambulatory Surgery Association

# About the Authors

## SCOTT BECKER

Mr. Becker, a partner resident in Ross & Hardies' Chicago office, practices exclusively in the area of health care. Mr. Becker provides counsel to ASCs, hospitals, pharmaceutical companies and providers, multi- and single-specialty medical practices and a wide variety of health care industry entrepreneurs. He provides service on a national basis with respect to health care transactional and regulatory matters, including Medicare/Medicaid fraud and abuse, tax exemption and related matters.

During the past several years, Mr. Becker has devoted most of his efforts to ASCs and specialty hospitals. His efforts include structuring ASC joint ventures and drafting and implementing private placements of ASC shares to physicians, providing counsel on anti-kickback, safe harbor, tax exemption and related issues, developing networks of surgical providers, procuring certificate of need (CON) determinations, reviewing reimbursement-related issues, reviewing antitrust issues, negotiating business contracts, drafting and implementing compliance plans, negotiating private equity investments, and providing advice and counsel on a broad range of business and legal issues relating to ambulatory surgery service providers.

Mr. Becker is the author and editor of three books: *Ambulatory Surgery Centers: Legal and Regulatory Issues*, *Health Care Law: A Practical Guide* and *The Physician's Managed Care Success Manual*. He is also the general editor of the *Matthew Bender Health Law Monthly* and an editor of the *Aspen Journal of Health Care Finance* and *Aspen's Inside Ambulatory Care*. He has authored and published more than 50 articles. Mr. Becker received his JD from Harvard Law School and is a graduate of the University of Illinois. He is also a certified public accountant.

## Scott Downing

Scott Downing, a partner in Ross & Hardies' Health Care Group, concentrates on corporate and regulatory health care matters with a focus on transactional issues such as mergers, acquisitions, joint ventures and the establishment of health care entities ranging from ASCs to multi- and single-specialty physician practices. Mr. Downing has participated in numerous transactions involving the purchase or sale of health care facilities and physician practices; negotiated and prepared physician employment agreements; counseled health care clients regarding compliance with the Medicare and Medicaid fraud and abuse laws, the Stark law, state fraud and abuse and self-referral acts, certificate of need issues, fee splitting and corporate practice of medicine issues.

Mr. Downing was associate editor of the Business Lawyer, an American Bar Association publication, for the 1993–1994 edition and received his JD from the University of Chicago. He is a graduate of the University of Illinois.

## Morgan Moran

Morgan Moran, an associate in Ross & Hardies' Chicago office, practices in the corporate health care group, where he focuses on mergers and acquisitions and general representation of health care providers. Mr. Moran's experience includes state licensure, formation and representation of for-profit and not-for-profit entities, assisting clients with multi-million-dollar asset sales, mergers and acquisitions. Mr. Moran counsels clients regarding compliance with and the interpretation of state health care laws.

Mr. Moran authored *Practitioner Licensure Issues in Telemedicine & Disease Management*, co-authored *OIG Advisory Opinions—1998 and 1999* and researched and contributed material for the Murer Consultants' 50-state survey book *The Complete Legal Guide to Healthcare Records Management*. Mr. Moran received his JD from the Chicago-Kent College of Law and is a graduate of the University of Wisconsin–Madison.

# CHAPTER 1

# Licensing and Certificate of Need Issues

Two state-specific questions must be addressed immediately for all ambulatory surgery center (ASC) projects—whether developments, acquisitions or expansions:

- Is a state license required?
- Is a certificate of need (CON) required?

## LICENSING

Nearly every state has licensing requirements for health care facilities, usually with specific requirements for ASCs. State licensing requirements vary greatly among the states, making it impossible to provide a useful description here. For example, California relies entirely on Medicare certification regulations as its criteria for licensure. On the other hand, Oklahoma has more than 30 pages of regulations and appendixes covering everything from medical records to janitors' closets. Topics that may be covered by state licensing requirements include building specifications, equipment (particularly safety or emergency equipment), staffing, processes for transferring patients to hospitals and billing procedures. The procedures that can be performed in an ASC may also be limited by the state licensing requirements. Some states limit ASCs to cases that do not require overnight recovery. Other states allow cases to be performed that require stays of more than 24 hours. Some states offer exemptions from all or some requirements to ASCs in physicians' offices, those of a limited size or those providing services in only one specialty. Prior to entering a contract to build, expand or significantly change an ASC, you need to determine whether or not a state license is needed and what requirements your state imposes on what the ASC can do and how it must be operated. In the

**Protecting Your ASC: A Legal Handbook**   1

planning stages, it is crucial that these requirements and limitations be understood.

One of the first steps in planning an ASC should be to obtain a copy of the state law(s) and regulations governing the licensing and operation of ASCs in your state. Once you've reviewed these documents, you may want to contact the state department that regulates ASCs with any questions regarding the requirements. Should you get specific interpretations, you should document the name, title and phone number of the person with whom you spoke and the date the conversation took place. You can ask the people you speak with to document their answers in writing, but state officials are often unwilling to do so. You may also want to contact your state's ASC association if one exists. Information on how to reach the relevant state officials, obtain copies of laws and regulations, and contact your state ASC association is available from FASA. Any issues that give you concern should be discussed with legal counsel.

# CERTIFICATE OF NEED LAWS

More than half the states have CON laws that may affect your ability to build or open a new ASC or to expand the size, equipment or services provided in an existing ASC. CON laws may also affect sales and other transactions involving the ASC. Thus, one of your initial steps in planning an ASC is to obtain information on whether or not your state has a CON law and, if so, what it requires. (For a list of states with CON laws, see appendix A.)

## EXEMPTIONS

If your state requires a CON for ASCs, you should determine whether or not there are exemptions to the CON requirements that are applicable to your ASC. Exemptions to CON requirements are often provided for a number of actions and situations, such as

- office practice–based surgery
- new projects below a specific dollar amount
- expansions and renovations below a certain amount or size
- relocations
- change of ownership

If attempting to qualify for an exemption, you should receive as much assurance as possible that the operation meets the exemption. The goal is to avoid a situation in which a challenge by a private party or the state pre-

---

2     Chapter 1 • Licensing and Certificate of Need Issues

vents the already-constructed ASC from being licensed, certified or used. For example, you may attempt to confirm in writing that the exemption is available and your plans qualify. However, even if an exemption letter is granted or confirmed, the issuance of the exemption letter may be challenged administratively or in court. Thus, the ASC's legal counsel must be able to defend the assertions and representations made in the initial request for an exemption. Accordingly, the ASC must be able to substantiate all facts and figures with the proper documentation (e.g., copies of contracts and agreements). Failure to do so may result in the recision of the exemption letter.

## OFFICE PRACTICE–BASED SURGERY

Many states do not require CONs for ASCs based in medical practices. Requirements to qualify for the exemption vary from state to state. Conditions often include that

- the ASC will not be Medicare certified,
- use will be limited to physicians affiliated with the practice,
- the number of operating rooms will not exceed a specified number,
- the dollar amount spent on facilities or equipment will not exceed a specific amount.

For example, Georgia permits an ASC to be built within a physican practice without a CON as long as the ASC is used by a single practice and expenditures to build the ASC are below $1 million.

Payers sometimes refuse to pay facility fees to such ASCs, arguing that it is a physician practice, not an ASC. One concern with using this exemption is whether or not enough payers will reimburse the ASC to make it profitable.

## NEW PROJECTS BELOW A SPECIFIC DOLLAR AMOUNT

Many states permit building an ASC without obtaining a CON if expenditures are below a certain limit. The expenditure limits vary widely from state to state. For example, in Delaware, projects under $5 million can be built without a CON. In Maine, however, a CON is required for new projects worth more than $100,000.

It is critical to understand what expenditures are counted toward the limit. For example, in many states, the ASC can exclude expenditures made by the landlord, expenditures for the shell of the building, expenditures that will be leased and operating expenditures. By carefully defining what is and what is not included in expenditure limits and confirming by

**Protecting Your ASC: A Legal Handbook**

letter such inclusions and exclusions with the state, it may be possible to build a much larger ASC without obtaining a CON than one may have anticipated. Developing the project on budget is critical in these situations.

## EXPANSIONS AND RENOVATIONS BELOW A CERTAIN DOLLAR AMOUNT OR SIZE

Significantly expanding services or renovating your ASC can trigger a new CON process in a number of states. In some states even adding new beds to your ASC requires a CON. Some states, however, allow expansion or renovation of an existing ASC without obtaining a new CON if the project is below a certain dollar amount. Tennessee, for example, requires a new CON if you spend $2 million or more on capital expenditures or $1 million or more on equipment. Illinois allows projects up to $6 million without a new CON.

## RELOCATIONS

CON laws can have an impact on your decision to move your ASC to a new location, as some states require a new CON to relocate an existing ASC. On the other hand, other states do not. Alaska's statute clearly states that ASCs can relocate without regard to the budget of the new facility as long as neither the bed capacity nor the number of categories of health services provided at the new site is greater than those at the original facility.

## CHANGE OF OWNERSHIP

CON laws can also have significant impact in the sale and transaction setting. In most states, once a party has a CON, they can sell or transfer the ASC and the new buyer will not need to obtain a new CON. Rather, the new buyer will only have to file certain forms and work through an abbreviated process with the state. However, because state laws vary, this should be explored when beginning discussions about sales.

## OBTAINING A CON

CON applications and processes differ greatly from state to state. Most states require that a letter of intent be filed before the actual CON application is filed. In some states, letters of intent can be submitted at any time. In other states, a strict schedule must be adhered to. For example, letters of intent must be filed by a certain date, and the application must be filed within a specified period of time after that.

State requirements vary on how specific the letter of intent must be. In certain states, the party applying for the CON is required to set forth in detail information about the intended ASC, such as the exact location, the number of operating rooms and the sources of financing. In other states, a more general statement informing the state of city location and preliminary plans will suffice at the letter of intent stage.

In addition to informing the state agency that an application will be forthcoming, the letter of intent alerts potential opposing parties to the CON that an application will be submitted. Based upon this advance knowledge, opposing parties can take action detrimental to the ASC. At the very least, opposing parties can begin preparations to oppose the application. They also may submit competing applications or amend their own plans to make your efforts to obtain a CON more difficult. For example, in states where hospitals are not restricted by CON requirements, a local hospital may announce a plan to expand or to open additional operating rooms, making it more difficult to show that there is a need for the additional operating rooms planned by the ASC.

## CRITERIA FOR NEED

The criteria used to judge a CON application also differ from state to state. A major difference is whether the state employs an objective standard or a subjective set of criteria to judge applications. States using an objective standard determine whether or not to grant a CON solely on a numeric calculation. This calculation can relate either to population per operating room or to the number of cases being performed per operating room in the CON area.

Alternatively, a state may use a more subjective set of criteria to judge CON applications. For example, CON applications in Connecticut are judged based upon the following principles and guidelines:

> The relationship of the proposal . . . to the state health plan; the relationship of the proposal . . . to the applicant's long-range plan; the financial feasibility of the proposal . . . and its impact on the applicant's rates and financial condition; the impact of such proposal . . . on the interests of consumers . . . and the payers . . . the contribution of such proposal . . . to quality, accessibility and cost-effectiveness of health care delivery in the region; . . . the relationship of any proposed change to the applicant's current utilization statistics; the teaching and research responsibilities of the applicant; the special characteristics of the patient-physician mix of the applicant; the voluntary efforts of the applicant in improving productivity and containing costs; and any other factors which the office deems relevant, including . . . such factors as, but not limited to, the business interests of all owners, partners, associates, incorporators, directors, sponsors, stockholders and operators. . . . [1]

**Protecting Your ASC: A Legal Handbook**

## CON APPLICATION – CORE CONCEPTS

A proponent for a CON in a state using subjective criteria should develop three or four core concepts that will serve as the main, or core, arguments in the application and throughout the hearing process for the CON. These core concepts will often relate to the ASC's ability to provide care at lower cost than in the hospital setting and the ability to ease overcrowding of area operating rooms. A mix of statistics, expert opinion, analysis and community support is most effective in making these arguments successfully. Tools used to support applications often include the following:

- letters from payers
- letters from local businesses
- support from physicians
- support from patients
- population data
- national health care and consulting experts
- case volume data
- price data
- indigent care service commitments
- maps demonstrating service area

Data are often obtained from private entities as well as from state and local government sources (e.g., FASA, the Centers for Medicare and Medicaid Services [CMS], SMG Marketing Group, Inc., and the US Census Bureau).

### LOWER COSTS

To demonstrate that the ASC will offer lower costs to patients and payers, the following items can be used:

- a comparison of invoices at local hospitals for outpatient procedures for the previous couple of years versus the expected price of services at the proposed ASC
- a comparison of copayments for Medicare patients for procedures performed at a hospital as opposed to procedures performed in an ASC[2]
- letters from payers and community groups indicating their expectation that an ASC will be able to provide lower-cost services than the current hospital providers

## EASING THE OVERCROWDING OF OPERATING ROOMS

A second core argument focuses on demonstrating that patients are forced to wait for surgery because operating rooms in the community are busy. Here, there is often flexibility in the use of assumptions as to what level of usage equals maximum capacity for operating rooms. As a general rule, demonstrating that operating rooms are busy is easy if more than 950 to 1,000 cases are being performed per operating room per year in the CON area. In contrast, if operating rooms are being used for less than 700 to 800 cases per year, it is hard to demonstrate a need based completely on the undercapacity of operating rooms. Another way of demonstrating capacity is to estimate the average minutes per case to available operating rooms in the area. By using the average minutes per case and the total hours that an operating room is open per year, you can demonstrate the capacity in cases per operating room in the community. This may allow you to demonstrate that operating rooms are near capacity and that the addition of operating rooms will not significantly reduce cases in existing rooms. For this demonstration, it may be important to distinguish between inpatient and outpatient rooms as inpatient rooms will have a long or average case time. For example, an inpatient case may take an average of 90 minutes to 120 minutes while an outpatient case may take only 40 to 50 minutes.

Factors that affect the calculation of operating room usage include the following:

- expected population growth
- number of cases per population
- elderly and non-elderly population mix
- percentage of cases that are outpatient

Discussing how an ASC can provide greater access to indigents can also be helpful.

## REVIEW OF ALTERNATIVES

A third possible CON concept is to argue that an ASC is the preferred expansion mode for the community. Here, it is typical to discuss key alternatives and then articulate why the ASC is the preferred approach. This discussion may focus on the distance to other ASCs, the costs of reconfiguring the hospital, the cost of outpatient surgery in the hospital, the alternative of a hospital-owned ASC and office-based surgery alternatives.

## Definition of CON Area

This is a critical issue in your success. If the state does not specifically define the CON planning area, you can define the area in a way favorable to your project. For example, by excluding an outlying community hospital that is not busy, usage of operating rooms in the area will be higher. Because of the amount of manipulation that has and can be been done with this type of data, many state planning boards have developed specific rules to guide calculations. For example, the state may set the radius for the CON planning area, dictate the number of minutes per case or specify the threshold number of cases per operating room that can be used in the calculation. For example, Illinois requires that all operating rooms within 30 minutes of the planned site be included in the data and calculations. You can still argue and attempt to demonstrate that certain operating rooms are really more than 30 minutes away.

## CON Granted

Usually, once a CON is granted, you may begin building. However, another party may contest the CON through an administrative appeal or by filing a lawsuit. Moving forward with development while the appeal is pending holds significant risk, as the CON decision could be reversed. For example, in 1999 the Mississippi Supreme Court reversed a decision that granted an ASC a CON in 1997.[3]

## CON Denied

If your CON is denied, your options depend on your state law. Your options may include an administrative appeal or resubmission of an amended application. Challenging the decision in court is usually an option. In some states it is routine to appeal and resubmit several times before being successful. In other states, a denial is rarely overturned. Local advice on this issue may be well worth the cost.

# Other Licenses

In addition to an ASC license, other federal, state or local licenses may be needed, depending on your state and exactly what services you provide.

# CLIA

ASCs performing any laboratory tests, even urine pregnancy tests or fingerstick blood glucose tests, need to comply with the federal Clinical

Laboratory Improvement Act (CLIA) and obtain a CLIA certificate. Washington and some parts of New York operate CLIA-exempt state programs, so ASCs in those states should check state law. CLIA requires any laboratory performing testing on specimens derived from a human being for purposes of providing diagnosis, treatment, etc., to enroll with the CLIA program, regardless of whether the laboratory receives payment from Medicare, Medicaid or any other third-party payer.

ASCs performing only certain basic tests, such as dipstick urinalysis, can obtain a CLIA waiver. Waived laboratories perform only tests that have been determined to be so simple that there is little risk of error. A list of waived tests, currently numbering 40, can be found at www.hcfa.gov/medicaid/clia/waivetbl.rtf. Waived laboratories must meet only the following requirements:

- enroll in the CLIA program
- pay applicable certificate fees biennially
- follow manufacturers' test instructions

Laboratories in which a physician, midlevel practitioner or dentist performs no tests other than certain microscopy procedures may be classified as a provider-performed microscopy (PPMP) laboratory. Laboratories with a PPMP certificate perform tests, using a microscope, during the course of a patient visit on specimens that are not easily transportable. The PPMP certificate also permits performance of waived tests.

PPMP facilities must meet only the following requirements under CLIA:

- enroll in the CLIA program
- pay applicable certificate fees biennially
- meet certain quality and administrative requirements

To enroll in the CLIA program, laboratories register with the state survey agency and pay a fee. Information on contacting the state survey agency is available at www.hcfa.gov/medicaid/clia/ssa-map.htm. Those applying for a waived or PPMP certificate do not need an inspection in advance but may be subject to future inspections.

Should your ASC perform tests requiring a regular CLIA certificate, the ASC should register with the state survey agency, pay fees, be surveyed (if applicable) and obtain a CLIA certificate.

If your ASC is only performing blood draws to be sent out for analysis, you do not need a CLIA certificate.

**Protecting Your ASC: A Legal Handbook**      9

## Pharmacy or Drug-Dispensing Licenses

Depending on your state law, you may need a pharmacy license to dispense drugs. In other states, you need a pharmacy license only if you will be distributing or selling drugs to be used outside your facility. If your ASC will be dispensing any controlled substances, you will need a federal Drug Enforcement Administration (DEA) license and number. In some states, the state law will require you to use the DEA number of your medical director.

## Local Licenses

Many cities or counties require a license to operate a business. The local Chamber of Commerce is a good source of information about the basic requirements for operating a business.

## Radiology

For ASCs using radiology, special state requirements may exist. Also, if you intend to bill Medicare for radiology codes, you will need to have a license as an independent diagnostic testing facility.

# Conclusion

The issues discussed in this chapter are crucial for opening your ASC and can greatly affect your ability to operate the ASC profitably once open. Accordingly, you cannot devote too much time at the outset to understanding what you need to do to obtain a state license and a CON if required. Planning well for these issues will ultimately save your ASC time and money and you much stress. This chapter provides only a general overview of the issues you may confront and should give you a basic understanding. Usually, you will have to hire experts in these fields to actually handle the issues for you. Given the importance of these issues, make sure your consultants are experts in these areas. Hiring consultants with ASC experience may save you time.

# CHAPTER 2

# Medicare Certification

Medicare will reimburse ASCs a facility fee for Current Procedural Terminology (CPT) codes on the ASC list. In 2001, this list contains just over 2,000 procedures. To be eligible for Medicare reimbursement, your ASC must be operated in conformance with Medicare conditions of coverage. These conditions cover virtually every aspect of ASC operations, including facility design, equipment needed, medical records, personnel and care delivery. In addition, ASCs must obtain Medicare certification to be reimbursed by Medicare. Obtaining Medicare certification can be a time-consuming and frustrating process, but planning early for this step will make it go more smoothly and efficiently. Achieving Medicare certification involves three main steps:

- operating your ASC in conformance with Medicare conditions of coverage
- obtaining a survey to show the Medicare program that you meet requirements for participation in the program as an ASC
- obtaining a provider number

## OPERATE IN CONFORMANCE WITH MEDICARE CONDITIONS OF COVERAGE

One of the conditions of receiving reimbursement is that the ASC be operated in accordance with Medicare's conditions of coverage for ASCs. A copy of these regulations is included in appendix B. Some of these conditions, such as those requiring that your facility be built in accordance with the Life Safety Code, are predominant issues as you build your ASC. Others, such as one requiring that you conduct an ongoing self-assessment of quality of care, will require your ongoing attention. If you are not experienced in ASC management, it is recommended that you read and re-read

**Protecting Your ASC: A Legal Handbook**                    **11**

these conditions regularly until you are thoroughly familiar with all the requirements. You will want to be sure that you are in compliance with all items before you have a surveyor come to determine compliance. Moreover, you will need to ensure that you remain in compliance as Medicare can re-inspect your facility any time.

## OBTAINING A SURVEY

Two options exist for Medicare surveys: a survey by a state agency or an accreditation body. Your ASC must be open and some procedures performed before you can be surveyed for Medicare compliance. The state dictates the number of procedures that must have been performed. If using the state agency, discuss scheduling with your state agency long before you open as there may be long waiting lists for surveys. Continue your interaction throughout the development of your ASC. Be sure you know exactly what you need to do for a state survey so that you will pass on the first attempt.

Three private accrediting bodies—the Accreditation Association for Ambulatory Health Care (AAAHC), the Joint Commission on Accreditation of Healthcare Organizations (JCAHO) and the American Association for Accreditation of Ambulatory Surgery Facilities, Inc. (AAAASF)—have been approved by CMS to determine whether or not ASCs are in compliance with Medicare's conditions of coverage. One of these accrediting agencies, in exchange for a fee paid by the ASC, serves as the surveying agency that determines whether or not the ASC complies with the Medicare conditions of coverage. If so, the ASC is granted *deemed status*. For deemed status surveys, the accrediting body applies the Medicare standards. Using an accrediting body often allows ASCs to move forward with Medicare certification in a timely manner. An ASC must still meet the state's licensure requirements unless the ASC is exempted from state licensure or the accrediting body also has deemed status for state licensure purposes.

Should you choose to become accredited, you must decide which body you wish to be accredited by. The next step is to obtain a copy of that organization's standards. Once you have a copy, you can make sure your facility operates in accordance with these standards. Most likely, you will need to develop some additional policies and procedures. A list of contact information for the deemed status organizations can be found at www.fasa.org.

12          Chapter 2 • Medicare Certification

# Obtaining a Medicare Provider Number

Once you receive notice that you are approved for Medicare, you can begin providing services to Medicare beneficiaries. However, Medicare will not reimburse you for these procedures until you have a Medicare provider number. Once Medicare issues you a provider number, you can be reimbursed for procedures provided after the approval was granted even if the procedures are provided before you receive your provider number. To begin, you complete the application, CMS Form 855, and submit it to the state survey agency. Once the application is submitted, you should shepherd the form through the bureaucratic channels to ensure timely processing. The actual process varies state by state; however, typically the state agency receives CMS Form 855 with the state licensing application. The state agency conducts its review (including any survey for licensing purposes) and forwards the application to the CMS regional office. The CMS regional office will often ask for additional information and attempt to verify certain information. Of late, many CMS regional offices have focused heavily on review of collections, billing arrangements and management. Often, the ASC will be asked to make changes to such agreements. Once the CMS regional office has completed its review, the regional office issues the provider number.

A number of observations can be made about the process. The process may be very slow, so getting applications in quickly is critical. Although the state agency may be included, different rules govern the process. Phone calls to state and federal agencies to understand the exact process can be extremely useful. Use great care in making sure the application is accurate and complete. Inaccurately completed applications may delay the processing of your application. Worse yet, they could later be the basis for false claims actions against the ASC with it being argued that since the initial application was inaccurate, all claims filed under the provider number are thus false claims. Once everything is filed, it is necessary to follow up continually with the agencies to keep the process moving. Expect to do some follow-up work on the application at the request of the carrier. Thus, any of the contracts should include the right to amend agreements to comply with carrier requests. Keep exact records of your processing in terms of filing, follow-up phone calls (including whom you spoke with, date and time) and follow-up correspondence. This information can be used to prod the agencies to act more quickly. Keep copies of all written correspondence.

**Protecting Your ASC: A Legal Handbook**

## CONCLUSION

It is important that you decide early in the development process whether you will seek Medicare reimbursement for services. If so, your ASC needs to be designed to meet all Medicare conditions of coverage. A thorough understanding of these requirements will help assure that you can obtain Medicare certification. Addressing the process for obtaining a Medicare provider number as you move forward will avoid long delays once open.

# CHAPTER 3

# Governance

The governing body of an ASC, like any other organization, has the responsibility for defining the organization's direction and ensuring its effectiveness. This body, which may be called the board of directors or board of managers, should consist of visionary leaders who bring both diligence and objectivity to their work, which is based in a strong foundation and commitment to the mission and values of the organization, as designed by the governing body. Federal and state statutes, Medicare regulations, the shareholder or operating agreement and accreditation standards all contain requirements for governing bodies.

Generally, the governing body has the responsibility to take all actions on behalf of the ASC in accord with a duty of loyalty and a duty of care. This means that those serving on the governing body must make decisions in a manner that is strictly for the business benefit of the ASC, not for themselves as individuals. This also means that all decisions should be supported by careful reasoning and analysis.

The ASC's operating or shareholder agreement typically sets forth the rules of how actions can be taken. For example, the operating or shareholder agreement may dictate that a majority of the governing body is required to approve actions, that an action may be taken only at a meeting, that actions may be taken by a written vote, that a supermajority vote (two-thirds, for example) may be required for certain actions, or that the approval of specified directors (such as those appointed by a tax-exempt hospital) is required.

The operating or shareholder agreement may also require that notice be given prior to the taking or voting on certain actions. For example, many operating agreements require that an action cannot be taken at a meeting unless prior written notice has been provided to the directors. This requirement is intended to give the directors time to prepare to discuss such issues and actions intelligently. In most situations, the governing body can act on

**Protecting Your ASC: A Legal Handbook**     **15**

a broad range of actions relative to the ASC. However, a handful of actions, such as amending the shareholder agreements, selling the ASC or entering into joint ventures, may require the vote of the shareholders. These actions are usually set forth either in the state law or in the operating or shareholder agreement. The governing body should have a clear understanding of which actions require shareholder or member approval and other requirements of organizing documents.

The governing body should keep accurate minutes of actions taken and discussed at meetings. A record of minutes is important to show that the actions were properly authorized and that the directors met their duty of carefully considering the actions to be taken. Whoever is responsible for these minutes should review with legal counsel what should be included in the minutes. Too much detail can be as harmful as too little. It may be a good idea to have legal counsel review minutes.

The governing body is responsible for making sure the ASC operates in compliance with all laws. Thus, the governing body should be kept abreast of legal developments under a whole variety of legal statutes that can affect the ASC.

The members of the governing body or officers, when taking action or signing documents on behalf of the ASC, should always indicate in what capacity they are acting, for example as an officer, director or manager of the ASC. It is important that they not give the impression to a third party that they are taking action in an individual capacity. Keeping this clear is intended to help limit the ability of a third party to sue them individually for actions taken on behalf of the ASC.

The failure to handle appropriately one's responsibilities as an officer, director or manager can lead to liability on a number of fronts. Shareholders may sue an officer or director for decreased value of their ASC interest if the directors do not take appropriate actions. Also, failure to comply with state or federal law may lead to individual liability for a director, officer or key employee. The ASC should maintain officer's and director's insurance to help protect the managers, directors and officers from liability from serving in such capacities.

For practical and operational purposes, many defined responsibilities may be delegated to the operational management of the ASC. However, it should always be remembered that the governing body remains responsible for the organization's operation and performance. Management should give the governing body regular updates on operations and compliance with laws.

## CONCLUSION

This section briefly summarizes certain responsibilities of officers, directors and managers and provides an overview of suggestions and guidance. Those serving on ASC governing bodies should be familiar with the federal and state laws and operating and/or shareholder agreements that affect their responsibilities. Only individuals who are committed to providing diligent efforts on behalf of the ASC should serve as officers, directors or managers.

18                                                          Chapter 3 • Governance

# CHAPTER 4

# Compliance Plans

Increasingly, compliance plans are used by entities to ensure compliance with all laws. Given the complexities of operating as a health care provider and the potential penalties for violating laws or government regulations, it is prudent for all health care entities to have a compliance plan. A compliance plan should focus on federal and state fraud and abuse laws, including those addressing false claims, kickbacks and referrals. It can also include labor and employment issues, corporate governance and a variety of other laws.

The principal goals of a compliance plan are to

- ensure compliance with all laws,
- demonstrate good faith intent toward compliance,
- limit penalties and sanctions in the event problems are found by a government body,
- educate employees as to legal compliance.

Establishing policies to ensure compliance with the law, educating employees about these policies and monitoring compliance with the law and the plan are the cornerstones of a compliance program. Although this chapter provides guidance about how to develop a compliance plan, including provisions to consider, legal advice should be sought in developing and implementing a compliance plan. This chapter focuses on a compliance plan relating to federal health care laws. State law provisions should also be considered. In addition, you should consider including provisions relating to compliance with other laws, such as those dealing with sexual harassment, discrimination and employee benefits. Employers have defeated employees' claims of sexual harassment because the employers had programs in place to help them learn about and address sexual harassment.

**Protecting Your ASC: A Legal Handbook**

# COMPLIANCE POLICIES

The ASC should develop written compliance policies regarding fraud and abuse issues that address specific areas of potential fraud, such as billing, contracting, marketing and claims processing. The compliance policies should be distributed to all individuals who are affected by the specific policy. A system should be used to file and retain these policies so that they are easily retrieved for reference. A discussion of some key provisions of a compliance plan follows.

# COMPLIANCE WITH THE LAW

Your compliance plan should begin with a statement that it is the ASC's policy to comply with all applicable federal and state laws and regulations. The statement could include an indication that this compliance plan is being adopted to ensure compliance.

# CHIEF COMPLIANCE OFFICER

A chief compliance officer is usually appointed to oversee the compliance program. Given the small number of employees at most ASCs, this person will have other duties as well. The chief compliance officer should report to the ASC's governing body. The chief compliance officer is responsible for

- developing compliance policies and standards;
- achieving compliance;
- overseeing and monitoring the ASC's compliance activities;
- ensuring that all compliance policies are kept up-to-date;
- ensuring that all employees are aware of and follow compliance policies;
- distributing compliance information in a form that is easily understandable to all employees;
- responding to, or identifying the appropriate person to respond to, all potential fraud and abuse problems or questions raised by employees;
- appointing employees as necessary to perform compliance functions.

# EMPLOYEE POLICIES

The ASC's employees are key to the success of any compliance plan. Accordingly, significant efforts should be devoted to being sure that all employees understand the ASC's policies, the importance of complying, how to comply and how to report violations.

In addition, the compliance plan needs to be integrated with the ASC's human resources policies, including a statement in human resource policies such as "strict compliance with compliance plan policies and requirements is a condition of employment for all employees." All applicants for jobs should be notified of this policy. When hired, all employees should be informed of the ASC's policy of strict compliance. Having employees sign an acknowledgment that they have been told of this policy and have been given a copy of the compliance plan may be helpful should disciplinary actions or termination be necessary. Moreover, such documentation could help demonstrate the ASC's seriousness about the compliance program and employee involvement if the ASC should be investigated for potential violations.

It is advisable to adopt a policy against retribution of any kind against an employee that reports suspected violations. Without such a policy, employees will be reluctant to report. Moreover, government entities typically look at such a policy as one element of a serious compliance plan.

Employees should be informed that compliance with all federal and state laws is a high priority for the ASC and that the employee is a critical part of this effort. All employees should be informed in writing that if they become aware of any of the following, the situation should be reported to the compliance officer or the compliance hotline, if one exists:

- remuneration offered to physicians
- any lease, purchase agreement or order for goods or services for any amount other than fair market value
- claims billed for an amount in excess of permitted rates, including double billing (billing two or more times for the same service or procedure) or balance billing Medicare patients (billing Medicare for a service or procedure and then billing the patient for the difference between the usual and customary charge and the amount that Medicare pays for the services)
- any medical claims or other service claims that are or may be false
- any other instance or potential instance of false claims or other fraud and abuse
- any violations of any federal or state laws or regulations

**Protecting Your ASC: A Legal Handbook**

Promotion of and adherence to the compliance plan should be an element in evaluating the performance of managers and supervisors. Managers and supervisors should be responsible for

- discussing with all supervised employees the compliance policies and legal requirements applicable to their functions,
- informing all supervised personnel that strict compliance with these policies and requirements is a condition of employment,
- disclosing to all supervised personnel that the ASC will take disciplinary action up to and including termination for violation of these policies or requirements.

Supervisory evaluations should take into consideration any situations in which supervisors and managers failed to instruct their subordinates adequately or failed to detect non-compliance with applicable policies and legal requirements, where reasonable diligence on the part of the supervisor or manager would have led to the discovery of any problems or violations and given the ASC the opportunity to correct them earlier.

Individuals who have been convicted of a criminal offense related to health care or who are listed by a federal agency as debarred, excluded or otherwise ineligible for participation in federally funded health care programs should not be employed by the ASC. (For a list of excluded individuals, see http://exclusions.org.home.html.)

Current employees who are charged with criminal offenses related to health care or proposed for exclusion or debarment should be removed from direct responsibility for or involvement in any federally funded health care program until resolution of such criminal charges or proposed debarment or exclusion. Human resources policies should include processes for handling such situations to ensure that the employee is treated fairly and that no labor laws are violated. If resolution results in conviction, debarment or exclusion of the individual, the ASC should terminate its employment of that individual.

## EDUCATING EMPLOYEES

The ASC should provide periodic educational and training programs on compliance with relevant laws to all employees, but especially to personnel involved in billing, sales, leasing, contracting, staffing, marketing and ordering of diagnostic tests or other laboratory work. Training should be conducted at least annually and repeated at regularly scheduled times using a variety of teaching methods, including various languages, as needed. Attendance should be required. These programs should be designed to

- emphasize the ASC's commitment to compliance with all laws, regulations and guidelines of federal and state programs,
- reinforce the fact that strict compliance with the law and the ASC's policies is a condition of employment,
- teach employees what practices and procedures are not allowed under the fraud and abuse statutes and what procedures should be used under the compliance policy,
- emphasize that employees raising potential violations will not suffer any retribution.

Because of the small number of employees in most ASCs, it may be more efficient to send employees to outside programs about compliance issues. However, such classes will not replace the need to provide information internally to educate employees about the ASC's particular policies, methods to report concerns and commitment to the compliance program.

Employees should be encouraged to ask about any questionable or confusing issues. Employees should be able to bring forward any information or questions without retribution and with complete anonymity. Employees should be assured that they will not face any penalties or other forms of retribution when they make any such reports.

# BILLING

The ASC should implement a system to ensure that all claims submitted to Medicare or other federally funded health care programs, state health care programs and private insurance are accurate and correctly identify the services or procedures ordered and performed. This system should include standardized billing and physician forms. When billing, the code that most accurately describes the service or procedure performed must be used. Use of any other code is potentially a false claim. Intentional upcoding or downcoding results in false claims and, thus, must not be done.

To avoid miscoding, the ASC should use only the information provided by the physician at the time of or specific to the service or procedure performed. Coders should not

- use information provided by the physician from earlier dates of service,
- use cheat sheets that provide information for what has resulted in reimbursement in the past,
- use computer programs that automatically insert codes without receipt of information from the physician,
- make up information for claims submission purposes.

**Protecting Your ASC: A Legal Handbook**

In addition, the ASC must bill only for those services and procedures that were actually performed. If there is a question as to what procedures were performed, the physician and other involved parties should be contacted before a service or procedure is billed.

Services or procedures should not be double billed. Audits should be used to investigate billing practices, including a review of double billing, balance billing, appropriate rates for billing and the billing of appropriate procedures.

## WAIVER OF COPAYMENTS AND DEDUCTIBLES

The ASC should have a policy on waivers of copayments and deductibles. Medicare regulations prohibit routine waivers of copayments and deductibles. For indigent Medicare patients, however, waivers can be considered. Even in this case, however, Medicare copayments and deductibles cannot be routinely waived. For other patients, state law should be consulted in establishing the appropriate policy. Private insurance contracts may also prohibit waivers of copayments and deductibles. Even if waivers are not prohibited by your insurance contract, insurance companies frown on them, and granting routine waivers may subject you to increased scrutiny.

## MEDICAL NECESSITY REQUIREMENT

The ASC should have a policy regarding billing federally funded health care programs only for medically necessary services and procedures. State health care programs and private insurance may also require medical necessity.

Because the physician orders the service or procedure, he or she bears the prime responsibility for determining medical necessity. However, the ASC submitting the bill is responsible for the bill being accurate in its entirety. The Medicare claim form contains specific language regarding the supplier certifying medical necessity. Specifically, CMS Form 1500 includes the following language: "I certify that the services listed above were medically indicated and necessary." Moreover, Medicare conditions of coverage for ASCs specifically require the ASC to conduct an "ongoing, comprehensive self-assessment of the quality of care provided, including medical necessity of procedures performed."

The ASC should take steps to ensure that the physicians understand Medicare's definition of medical necessity and that Medicare will be billed for only those services or procedures that are medically necessary. Specifically, the ASC should

- inform physicians which services or procedures are covered by Medicare in the ASC;
- provide physicians with written notices annually, or more often if required, that set forth the ASC's medical necessity policy;
- develop physician order forms requiring physicians to document the need for each service or procedure performed, inserting the appropriate code for each of those services or procedures. These forms should include a statement that only medically necessary services and procedures will be billed to federally or state-funded programs or to insurers.

However you do it, you need some mechanism for documenting the medical necessity of the procedures you perform.

You may want to consider requiring physicians to sign physician acknowledgment forms in which they affirm such items as their understanding that Medicare will pay only for a medically necessary service or procedure and their agreement with key elements of the ASC's policy on medical necessity.

# MARKETING AND REFERRALS

All marketing done on the ASC's behalf should be honest, straightforward, fully informative and non-deceptive. Physicians and other providers should fully understand the services offered by the ASC and the financial consequences for Medicare, as well as other payers, for the services provided. The compliance plan can include an approval process for marketing materials and plans to assure that they comply with all laws.

No remuneration should be given to induce or encourage a physician or other provider to use the ASC. This means there should not be any kind of payment, including kickbacks, bribes or rebates, either in cash or in kind, in any manner or form to any physician or other party to induce the referrals of any health care business, patients, or other items or services to the ASC. For example:

- Any agreement with any physician or other party that may refer business to the ASC should be reviewed and approved in advance by someone who is knowledgeable about legal requirements, for example, the chief compliance officer or legal counsel. These agreements include leases, purchases or orders.
- If any payments are made to a physician to reduce or limit services offered to a Medicare beneficiary or a beneficiary of other federal or state programs, they should be reported and approved.

**Protecting Your ASC: A Legal Handbook**

- ASCs should not be required or expected to refer Medicare and/or Medicaid business to any of their business affiliates. Employees should be required to report any such suggestions by business affiliates to the chief compliance officer.

## ASC RELATIONSHIPS WITH LABORATORIES AND OTHER PROVIDERS

The ASC should consider monitoring laboratory and other agreements with entities providing services to the ASC or its patients to ensure that there are no fraud and abuse or Stark law violations. Specifically, the policy could require the chief compliance officer to examine such relationships to ensure that they reflect fair market value and are not tied to referrals or intended to ensure cross-referrals.

## RECORD CREATION AND RETENTION

The compliance plan should state that all records required by either federal or state law shall be appropriately created and maintained. Where patient confidentiality will not be compromised, reports summarizing the records should be created and maintained. If there is any question as to whether or not patient confidentiality will be compromised, legal counsel should be consulted.

## ADVISORY OPINIONS

An evolving part of compliance efforts is to request advisory opinions from federal or state authorities. On a federal level, the Department of Health and Human Services, Office of Inspector General (OIG) and the Internal Revenue Service (IRS) have processes that those involved in a transaction or potential transactions can use to inquire as to whether or not a relationship or transaction complies with certain laws. In general and as part of a compliance program, it is becoming increasingly common to request guidance of the OIG regarding Stark and anti-kickback issues. It has also been common for a long time to request IRS guidance in the form of private letter rulings.

# Monitoring Compliance

The ASC should monitor the implementation of its compliance plan and report regularly to senior executives and the governing body. The monitoring functions should include

- regular internal checks on procedures, relationships and actions;
- periodic independent third-party reviews or audits;
- a hotline for reporting all improper conduct, preferably anonymously;
- background checks on candidates before they are hired;
- periodic review of compliance efforts by the governing body;
- periodic updates of legal changes to the governing body;
- regular updates to the governing body on compliance efforts.

Third-party reviews or audits are designed to ensure compliance with the ASC's compliance plan and policies and all federal and state laws. Audits can also address issues related to contracts, competitive practices, marketing materials, coding and billing, reporting and record keeping. The audit process may include

- on-site visits;
- interviews with personnel involved in management, operations, billing, sales, marketing, referrals and other related activities;
- review of materials and documentation used by the ASC;
- billing and coding analyses and audits.

The audit reports should specifically identify areas where corrective actions are needed. The audit reports should be thoroughly reviewed and appropriate corrective measures taken if necessary. Follow-up audits should be conducted to ensure that the corrective measures were implemented and remedied the situation.

Anonymous hotlines for employees to use to report suspected violations are also highly recommended. For ASCs that have few employees and are not a part of a network, operation of an internal hotline might prove costly, is unlikely to be seen by the staff as providing anonymity and will be difficult to operate in a professional way. Another alternative is to subscribe to a service that operates a hotline and provides reports of any calls to whomever you direct, for example, the ASC Hotline available through FASA.

**Protecting Your ASC: A Legal Handbook**

# INVESTIGATION OF ALLEGED VIOLATIONS

The ASC should have a policy to promptly investigate any potential violations or misconduct to determine whether or not a violation has in fact occurred and, if so, what steps to take to rectify it; to report it to the government, if appropriate; and to make any appropriate payments to the government. This includes all matters reported by employees. Depending on the nature of the allegations, the investigations should include interviews and review of relevant documents, such as submitted claims, procedure and service order forms, and medical reports. If reasonable, the chief compliance officer should engage outside auditors or counsel to assist in the investigation. One factor in determining whether or not to use outside legal counsel to conduct the investigation is that using legal counsel may allow protection of some or all of the records and indexes of the investigation under the attorney-client privilege. Because the laws governing this vary widely, you should consult with your legal counsel on this element of your compliance plan.

If the integrity of the investigation is at stake because of the presence of one or more employees under investigation, those allegedly involved in the misconduct can be removed from their current work activity until the investigation is completed. Policies on whether or not these individuals may work in other positions, salary and benefits should be delineated in the plan. In addition, the chief compliance officer should take steps to prevent the destruction of documents or other evidence relevant to the investigation. Once an investigation is completed, if disciplinary action is warranted, it should be immediate, in accordance with appropriate personnel policies and labor laws.

# MODIFICATION OF THE COMPLIANCE PLAN

The ASC should modify its compliance plan as necessary to maintain compliance with state and federal fraud and abuse laws as they are amended. Sending employees to industry programs and subscribing to industry publications, such as *Ambulatory Surgery Compliance and Reimbursement Insider*, will help identify areas for modification.

## CONCLUSION

This review of basic compliance plan provisions provides a good overview of how to develop a compliance plan. To be most effective, you will need to start with these provisions and draft your own provisions to reflect the unique nature of your facility. The most important point to remember is that a compliance plan is not something that is drafted and put on the shelf. For your ASC to benefit from your compliance plan, it needs to be used by management and employees regularly. All employees should feel that it is a source to cite when questions or concerns arise. Equally important, as issues arise or laws change, the plan needs to be modified.

30                                                    Chapter 4  •  Compliance Plans

# CHAPTER 5

# Medical Staff Credentialing and Privileging

As a health care facility, one of the most important functions of the ASC is to determine which health care professionals can provide services in the ASC, what procedures they can perform and the conditions under which these procedures can be performed. Medicare regulations require that members of the medical staff "be legally and professionally qualified for the positions to which they are appointed and for the performance of privileges granted." Qualifications are determined by the medical staff credentialing and privileging process. Credentialing is the process of granting a health care professional the ability to provide services in the ASC. Privileging defines which procedures the individual can perform. Although usually done at the same time, it is critical that the process have two components. The primary goal of credentialing and privileging is to ensure that the physicians and other health care professionals practicing in the facility are of high quality and perform only those procedures that they are qualified to perform. Thus, the credentialing and privileging process is the cornerstone of the ASC's quality program.

## PROCESS FOR CREDENTIALING AND PRIVILEGING

The medical staff bylaws govern credentialing and privileging. The medical staff bylaws should establish a process for credentialing and for granting, revoking or changing privileges. This process must be consistently adhered to for all medical staff members. Although usually referred to as medical staff privileging, it should apply to any health care professional providing independent patient care. Your medical staff bylaws should require periodic recredentialing of those on the medical staff. Periodic recredentialing is a Medicare requirement.

Protecting Your ASC: A Legal Handbook                                                      31

All those seeking credentials to perform procedures in the ASC should be required to file an application. The application should gather the information needed to verify all the appropriate credentials of applicants. This information includes basic identifying information, such as legal name; address; Social Security number; information relevant to the ability to practice medicine, such as medical school, residencies attended, state license information and DEA license, if applicable; and information on privileges sought, such as training and hospital privileges. In addition, a malpractice history should be sought. If the ASC requires medical staff to have liability insurance, the applicant should provide documentation of coverage. The application should also include questions about health status. Inquiries should be made as to board certification, cardiopulmonary resuscitation (CPR) certification and advanced cardiac life support (ACLS) certification. The application should require a signature and a statement certifying that all the information given is true to the best of the applicant's knowledge. You may also want to include a statement that submission of false information is grounds for denial of credentials or revocation if discovered after credentials are granted.

The ASC's bylaws should require verification of specific information and assign responsibility for such verification. This responsibility can be delegated to ASC staff. Key information, such as medical licenses, should be verified using primary sources. The National Practitioner Data Bank (NPDB) should be checked regarding malpractice history and any potential adverse actions by other health care entities. Information in the NPDB can be accessed directly upon an application and payment of a fee. Contact the NPDB at www.npdb.com to become a querying entity. Alternatively, applicants can be required to submit queries on themselves and provide the original reports they obtain from the NPDB with their applications. The Federation of State Medical Boards has a database of state licensing actions. Checking this source can verify whether or not the physician has had actions taken against him or her in any state. Access this information at www.docinfo.org. You should verify that the applicant has not been excluded from participation in the Medicare or Medicaid program at http://exclusions.oig.hhs.gov/html.

Once the appropriate information has been verified, the application and verification information is ready for action. The medical staff bylaws should establish a medical staff committee to review all applications for credentials and privilege questions. This committee ensures that all applications are reviewed by those in the ASC with clinical knowledge. Moreover, the Medicare regulations require that "[t]he ASC grants privileges in accor-

32          Chapter 5 • Medical Staff Credentialing and Privileging

dance with recommendations from qualified medical personnel." Based upon this factual review, the medical staff committee makes recommendations to the governing body. The governing body has overall responsibility for the ASC and must make the final decision on credentialing and privileging. Medicare regulations also require that the governing board make final decisions on credentialing and privileging. The medical staff committee should provide written recommendations to the governing body. The bylaws should specify that this process is designed to ensure quality, and decisions about credentials and privileges should be made solely on quality issues and not unrelated factors such as competition or other financial considerations. When considering an action involving a particular type of specialist, it may be desirable to use independent third-party practitioners to assist in reviewing the issues raised. For example, if the issues relate to an ophthalmologist, rather than using local competing ophthalmologists to assess the quality and competency of the physician, using an ophthalmologist who does not practice in the local area may add the appearance of impartiality to the process. While using a competitor does not necessarily mean that actions will not be immune from liability, it is often viewed as evidence that a party did not act in good faith in peer review or credentialing proceedings.

Items that should be given special attention in drafting bylaws include the circumstances under which an applicant has a right to a hearing and the right to an attorney and to issues such as the use of verbatim transcripts. Bylaws should clearly indicate which rights apply to which practitioners and which actions. The bylaws may establish different procedures and rules for those who are already on medical staff as compared with those seeking new appointments. A member of the medical staff usually has the right to legal counsel and a hearing when one of the following events occurs: (1) denial of requested advancement in medical staff membership; (2) denial of medical staff reappointment; (3) demotion to lower staff category; (4) suspension of medical staff membership; (5) expulsion from medical staff membership; (6) reduction in privileges; (7) suspension of privileges; (8) termination of privileges; or (9) denial of increase in privileges.

Moreover, those ASC actions that are not intended to give rise to rights to adversely affected individuals should clearly be articulated. For example, under properly drafted bylaws, a health care professional who loses the ability to practice at the ASC because an exclusive contract is granted to someone else may not have the right to bring action. A Texas court upheld this right saying that the hospital, through its bylaws, did not "guarantee work for any physician" nor did it "limit its rights to enter into exclusive

**Protecting Your ASC: A Legal Handbook**

contracts" and to generally conduct the business of the hospital. The court explained its decision saying:

> For example, if the Hospital chose to eliminate treatment of some specialty from the Hospital, the prior granting of staff privileges would not by implication prohibit the Hospital from making that business decision. While in the present case, the exclusive contract may have the effect of eliminating Gonzalez's work in the Hospital, it does not reduce or alter his staff privileges as such.[4]

The bylaws should delineate clear procedures for hearings, including whether or not the person requesting the hearing must be in attendance, whether or not the person may have an attorney present, whether or not formal rules of evidence are to be followed, whether or not there will be a verbatim transcript, who will be on the hearing committee, whether or not the committee will consist solely of active medical staff and who will bear the responsibility for costs.

The credentialing and privileges program should seek to limit to the greatest extent possible the disclosure of information generated or talked about in peer review settings and privileged discussions. This is a particularly important issue to the physicians serving on the medical staff committee. In that regard, the bylaws should include a provision stating that the ASC intends to provide participants to the process broad immunity and clearly set forth the intent that communications in meetings and between participants be privileged.

# LEGAL ISSUES

Although the primary purpose of your credentialing and privileging process is to ensure quality, legal issues should be considered as the process is developed and implemented because the ASC can be subjected to lawsuits stemming from this process. Legal counsel should be consulted so that the process is designed to limit its potential liability. One potential source of legal actions can be patients injured at the facility alleging that the ASC permitted unqualified physicians or other unqualified health care professionals to perform services in the ASC. Generally, a facility is not liable for the negligence of the independent staff member physicians. However, the ASC can be liable if it fails to credential physicians appropriately and thus allows physicians without the appropriate skills or qualifications to practice. For example, courts have held that a hospital or ASC has a direct "duty to use reasonable care in formulating the policies and procedures that govern its medical staff and non-physician personnel; and a duty to exercise reasonable care in the selection of its medical staff and to periodically monitor and review the medical staff's competence."[5]

A second type of legal risk is that those who are denied credentials or whose privileges are more limited than those sought will sue the ASC. These suits may be based upon a variety of legal theories. For example, minority health care professionals have brought lawsuits alleging discrimination. Other lawsuits have alleged antitrust issues.

In addition to the ASC being sued for actions taken, individual participants in the process could be sued. As a general rule, medical staff and employees participating in peer review processes, including credentialing and privileging discussions, cannot be held liable for their actions as long as they acted in good faith in furtherance of health care quality for the benefit of the facility and without malice. For example, the Texas Medical Practice Act provides that

> [a] cause of action does not accrue against a member, agent, or employee of a medical peer review committee or against the health-care entity from any act, statement, determination or recommendation made, or act reported, without malice, in the course of medical peer review.[6]

Malice and good faith in the peer review context have been interpreted to mean that the individual is acting with a reasonable belief that what he or she is stating is true and that he or she is not acting recklessly. The ability to challenge actions taken in the peer review context and impose liability on the parties involved, called *piercing of protective immunity*, can be greatly enhanced when those involved take certain actions such as making comments that cannot be readily supported. For example, in one case, an owner administrator was alleged to have called the physician concerned a "murderer." Because it could not be specifically substantiated that the physician was a "murderer," the owner administrator was deemed to forfeit the "immunity" from liability and thus could be sued. In another situation, a physician was found to be potentially culpable because he made statements that potentially could not be supported. The court in that case said a defendant can not:

> automatically insure a favorable verdict by testifying that he published with a belief that the statements were true. The finder of fact must determine whether or not the publication was indeed made in good faith. Professions of good faith will be unlikely to prove persuasive, for example, where a story is fabricated by the defendant, is the product of his imagination, or is based wholly on the unverified anonymous telephone call.[7]

In certain situations physicians have lost their immunity from civil suit by discussing aspects of the situation outside of the specific committee process. To avoid this possibility, the ASC should provide that all physicians, employees and others involved in credentialing, privileging and peer review processes be clearly instructed to discuss matters related to such issues only in the appropriate committee and peer review setting.

**Protecting Your ASC: A Legal Handbook**

Moreover, such instruction should be reiterated at the beginning of each meeting. In other situations, physicians have been held liable for their actions in the peer review context where they have taken action that has not been specifically endorsed or approved by the committee. To avoid this situation, when the medical director or administrator takes action in furtherance of the credentialing, privileging or peer review functions, wherever possible, he or she should take only action that has been approved specifically by the relevant committee and only the action documented. Moreover, the guidelines set forth in the committee's decisions should be strictly followed as parties have also been found liable in instances where they have not followed the specific medical staff bylaws to the letter.

## INFORMATION SOURCES

Given the significant legal risks associated with credentialing and privileging, you will want to consult your lawyer in developing the process. In designing a process, state law should be reviewed as it often sets out specific processes to be followed and may grant specific rights to the applicant or practitioner involved. In addition, the federal Health Care Quality Improvement Act of 1986 limits liability if certain processes are followed. However, legal issues are only a small part of this process, and accordingly, the ASC administrator, the medical staff and the governing body need to be actively involved in its development. As noted in several places, the Medicare regulations have several references to credentialing and privileging. The accrediting bodies have similar requirements and provide more specificity. If accreditation will be sought, you should review the specific requirements for the accrediting body that will be used and design your credentialing and privileging process to meet these requirements. If accreditation will not be sought, these requirements can still be used for guidance on how to establish a meaningful process.

## CONCLUSION

This chapter generally covers the requirements for a legal and effective credentialing and privileging process. However, this is clearly not a complete discussion of the subject. If you are not familiar with the topic, you should consult other sources or a consultant in developing your process. Although legal requirements apply to the process, legal issues are only one aspect of the credentialing and privileging process. A properly designed process should not only protect the ASC from legal action but also assist you in providing high-quality services.

# CHAPTER 6

# Employment Law Issues

Labor laws, as much as any other set of laws, have a day-to-day impact on how the ASC is operated. In addition to understanding a number of rules that should come with common sense (i.e., one cannot discriminate against employees based on race or religion), understanding the technical requirements of these statutes is critical. For example, under certain circumstances, an ASC must give employees the right to continuation of health care coverage (COBRA coverage) and notice of this right in a certain form and within a specified time frame. Under the Americans with Disabilities Act (ADA), a self-evaluation of policies is required. Further, you must keep a list of interested persons consulted in conducting this evaluation. These examples demonstrate the diversity and nature of these requirements. This chapter provides an overview of the issues raised by federal labor laws affecting the ASC arena.

Although state labor law often mirrors federal law, the state law may expand coverage beyond that of federal law or may impose additional requirements. Thus, you should also consult a good source of information on state law.

Moreover, labor laws are extremely complex and involve many core interrelations and detail well beyond the scope of this book. When dealing with a specific issue, it is prudent to consult an attorney experienced in labor law in your state.

## WAGES AND TIME OFF

The Fair Labor Standards Act of 1938 and subsequent amendments establishes a minimum hourly rate of pay for covered employees. It also provides for mandated overtime pay at the rate of not less than time and a half the regular rate if a person works more than 40 hours in a workweek. Additional provisions require that employees receive periodic breaks and

**Protecting Your ASC: A Legal Handbook**　　　　**37**

time off in certain periods. Ability to allow time off in exchange for over-time worked is extremely limited. In general, the time off must be taken in the same pay period as the overtime worked. Moreover, if the pay would have been at time and a half, the time off must be granted at time and a half. Certain kinds of administrators, professionals and executives are exempt from these overtime requirements. Your personnel system should specify which employees are classified as exempt. Consult the law in making these determinations.

The Equal Pay Amendment, enacted in 1963, prohibits an employer from discriminating between employees on the basis of sex by paying unequal wages to men and women who perform equal work on jobs that require equal skill, effort and responsibility and that are performed under similar working conditions. An exception exists for payment made pursuant to a seniority system, a merit system, a system that measures earnings by quantity or quality of production, or a differential based on any factor other than sex.

Federal law requires that you allow employees time off to serve on a jury. Most state laws have similar requirements and may also require time off for employees serving as witnesses. You do not have to pay employees for time spent on jury duty, but many employers do. Under certain circumstances, some states also require employers to provide time off for voting.

The federal Uniformed Services Employment and Reemployment Rights Act (USERRA) provides basic job protections to individuals serving in the uniformed services, including the Coast Guard, the commissioned corps of the Public Health Service, the reserves and the Army and Air National Guard. These rights accrue whether the service is voluntary or involuntary. Following service, the employer must reemploy the individual if he or she (1) had a job immediately prior to the military leave, (2) provided notice if there was an opportunity to do so, (3) took leave that did not exceed five years (although there are some exceptions to this), (4) received an honorary discharge, and (5) reported back to work in a timely manner. In addition to the job, the person completing military service must be given the seniority and pay that he or she would have had without taking the time out for military service. The law also requires certain employee benefits to be continued. Requirements vary by the type of benefit and length of service. Many employers provide protections and benefits beyond what is required. You may want to address this issue in your human resources policies and procedures. If you do not address these issues in advance and have an employee who is absent due to service in one of the above bodies, you will want to consult the law to assure that you comply with its requirements.

Chapter 6 • Employment Law Issues

# DISCRIMINATION

In addition to the prohibition on discrimination mentioned above, federal laws address discrimination based on race, age, sex, religion, national origin and disability. Race discrimination in private and public sector employment has been prohibited since 1866. Title VII of the Civil Rights Act makes it unlawful to (1) fail or refuse to hire or to discharge any individual, or otherwise to discriminate against any individual with respect to his compensation, terms, conditions or privileges of employment because of such individual's race, color, religion, sex or national origin; or (2) limit, segregate or classify employees or applicants for employment in any way that would deprive or tend to deprive any individual of employment opportunities or otherwise adversely affect his or her status as an employee, because of such individual's race, color, religion, sex or national origin.

Title VII also prohibits an employer from retaliating against an employee because the employee has (1) opposed practices made unlawful under this law or (2) filed a charge, testified, assisted or participated in an investigation, proceeding or hearing under this law. Title VII further prohibits an employer from advertising for employees in a way "indicating any preference, limitation, specification, or discrimination, based on race, color, religion, sex, or national origin" except when "religion, sex, or national origin is a bona fide occupational qualification for employment." Finally, Title VII prohibits discrimination in hiring or firing or by otherwise adversely affecting the employment status of an individual because of pregnancy. Title VII outlaws not only intentional discrimination but also policies neutral on their face that have a discriminatory effect.

The Age Discrimination in Employment Act of 1967 prohibits discrimination based on age for persons who are at least 40 years of age. An exception exists "where age is a bona fide occupational qualification reasonably necessary to the normal operation of the particular business." Also exempted is "a bona fide seniority system or any bona fide employee benefit plan such as a retirement, pension, or insurance plan, which is not a subterfuge to evade the purposes of" law. Employers are permitted to use a bona fide seniority system, provided the system does not permit involuntary retirement because of age. Minimum standards exist for determining the validity of waivers of rights under this law.

Section 503 of the Rehabilitation Act of 1973 requires employers who enter into government contracts or subcontracts for more than $10,000 to take affirmative action to employ and advance in employment qualified individuals with handicaps. The term *individual with handicap* for this purpose is defined as "any person who (i) has a physical or mental impair-

**Protecting Your ASC: A Legal Handbook**

ment which substantially limits one or more of such person's major life activities, (ii) has a record of such impairment, or (iii) is regarded as having such impairment." Specifically excluded is "an individual who is currently engaging in the illegal use of drugs" when the employer acts on the basis of such use. The required affirmative action program must include (1) a review of personnel procedures to ensure that handicapped applicants and employees receive full consideration and (2) a review of all physical or mental job qualification requirements to ensure that to the extent they tend to screen out handicapped individuals, they are job related and justified by business necessity. The fact that this review occurred should be documented in your records. Regulations further require covered employers to "make a reasonable accommodation to the physical and mental limitations of an employee or applicant unless the contractor can demonstrate that such an accommodation would impose an undue hardship on the conduct of the contractor's business." Covered employers are health care institutions that hold government contracts or subcontracts for $2,500 or more.

Section 504 of the Rehabilitation Act of 1974 prohibits discrimination on the basis of handicap by any employer receiving federal financial assistance. Receipt of Medicare or Medicaid reimbursement is generally found to qualify as federal financial assistance for this purpose. Moreover, if any one part of a health care institution receives federal financial assistance, the entire institution is covered. Department of Health and Human Services (HHS) regulations implementing Section 504 require covered employers to perform a self-evaluation of policies and practices. Those with 15 or more employees must also maintain on file the following: a list of interested persons consulted; a description of areas examined and problems identified; and a description of any modifications made or remedial steps taken. Covered employers also are required to notify employees, applicants and unions that they do not discriminate against handicapped individuals and to adopt a grievance procedure for employees alleging any prohibited action against the handicapped. Moreover, all covered employees are required to make reasonable accommodation for handicapped applicants and employees unless they can demonstrate that such accommodation would impose undue hardship.

Discrimination against former drug abusers due to their former addiction, as well as discrimination based on participation in rehabilitation programs or the erroneous perception of drug use, is prohibited. The term *individual with a disability* does not include any employee or applicant who currently engages in the illegal use of drugs when an employer acts on the basis of such use. It does include anyone who is participating in or has successfully completed a supervised drug rehabilitation program (or has otherwise been rehabilitated) and is no longer engaging in such use, as well as anyone erroneously regarded as engaging in such use. An alcoholic may qualify as an individual with a disability under the ADA and thus be protected from discrimination, but the ADA recognizes an employer's right to (1) prohibit the use of alcohol at the workplace; (2) require that all employees not be under the influence of alcohol at the workplace; and (3) hold an alcoholic employee to the same standards as other employees.

The ADA makes clear that infection with the human immunodeficiency virus (HIV) is a disability; thus, persons with HIV cannot be discriminated against.

The Vietnam Era Veterans' Readjustment Act of 1974 requires that any government contract or subcontract in the amount of $10,000 for the procurement of personal property and non-personal services, including construction, shall require the contracting party to take affirmative action to employ and advance "qualified special disabled veterans and veterans of the Vietnam era." The Vietnam Era Veterans' Readjustment Act also protects the employment and reemployment rights of veterans and reservists and National Guardsmen called into active duty. Amendments to this act following the Persian Gulf war clarify and extend these rights. Health care employers should be aware of their revised obligations to veterans.

Employers are prohibited from employing illegal aliens under the Immigration Reform and Control Act of 1986 (IRCA). IRCA requires employers to verify the identity and employment authorization of each employee hired after November 6, 1986, to work in the US. All employees must fill out a federal Department of Justice I-9 form, which can be obtained from www.doj.gov, within three days of beginning work. The employer must verify citizenship or right to work using specified documentation listed on the form. These records must be kept for three years from date of hire or one year after employment ends, whichever is greater. Penalties of $1,000 per hire can be imposed for failure to do so.

IRCA also prohibits employers with more than three employees from discriminating against any individual (other than an unauthorized alien) with respect to the hiring or recruitment of the individual for employment or the discharging of the individual from employment (1) because of such individual's national origin, or (2) in the case of a citizen or intending citizen, because of such individual's citizenship status. It is not unlawful, however, to prefer a US citizen or national over an alien if the two individuals are equally qualified.

# OCCUPATIONAL SAFETY AND HEALTH ACT

Under the Occupational Safety and Health Act (OSHA), ASCs, like all employers, have a general duty to furnish employees a place of employment free from recognized hazards that are likely to cause death or serious physical harm. OSHA conducts inspections if there is a complaint filed by employees or may do so on its own.

ASCs with more than 10 employees must maintain OSHA-specified records of job-related injuries and illnesses, referred to as OSHA Form 200 and OSHA Form 101.

The OSHA Form 200 is an injury/illness log, with a separate line entry for each work-related death, injury or illness that requires medical treatment (other than just first aid) and involves loss of consciousness, restriction of work or motion, or a transfer to another job. A summary section of the OSHA Form 200 must be posted in the workplace for the entire month of February each year. The OSHA Form 101 is an individual incident report that provides added detail about each individual death, injury or illness described above. A suitable insurance or workers' compensation form that provides the same details may be substituted for the OSHA Form 101.

In the rare circumstance that an employee fatality occurs or three or more employees are hospitalized due to a work-related accident, the nearest OSHA office must be notified within eight hours. OSHA prohibits discrimination against an employee who exercises any right created by the act.

In addition to the requirements applicable to all employees, OSHA has specific provisions dealing with health care providers. These very specific requirements include addressing the use of safe needles, procedures for dealing with contaminated wastes and use of barriers. These requirements are updated periodically so the latest requirements should be reviewed. As this book goes to press, OSHA is considering new standards to protect workers from exposure to tuberculosis and smoke plume from lasers, for example.

# EMPLOYEE RETIREMENT INCOME SECURITY ACT

ASCs generally offer employees some type of benefit plans such as retirement or pension plans. Those who do so will need to comply with the Employee Retirement Income Security Act (ERISA) and any state laws that govern such activities. ERISA sets minimum standards to make sure employee benefit plans are established and maintained in a fair and financially sound manner, which includes providing the promised benefits. Participants in the plan must be provided a summary plan description (SPD) describing, in understandable terms, their rights, benefits and responsibilities under the plan. Participants must be notified of changes to the plan. Copies of these documents must be furnished to the Department of Labor upon request.

Employers with more than 20 employees on a typical working day in the previous calendar year must give covered employees a notice informing them of their rights under the Consolidated Omnibus Budget Reconciliation Act of 1985 (COBRA) and describing the law. Basically, COBRA requires that employers offer continuing coverage to qualified beneficiaries under certain qualifying events. Qualified events that trigger a covered employer's obligation to offer the continuation coverage include (1) the termination of employment (for reasons other than gross misconduct); (2) a reduction in hours so that the employee no longer qualifies for regular insurance coverage; (3) the covered employee's death; (4) the divorce or legal separation of the covered employee from his or her spouse; (5) the covered employee's enrollment in Medicare; (6) the cessation of coverage of a dependent child under the terms of the plan; or (7) the bankruptcy of the employer (this applies only to retirees). Once a qualifying event has occurred, the employer must notify the qualified beneficiaries of their right to continue health care coverage at their own expense for between 18 and 36 months, depending on the type of qualifying event. If you use an outside plan administrator, he or she will generally handle these duties. You should make sure your contract requires that he or she does so and that you provide them with timely notification of all employee changes so that notices can be given within the legal requirements. If you plan to administer employee benefits in-house, you should consult with experts in the field in setting up the plan and ensuring you are familiar with all obligations. See also page 58. addressing issues of the relationship of physician owner benefit plans to those of the ASC.

It is important to note that ERISA makes it unlawful to discharge, discipline or discriminate against a participant or beneficiary for exercising any right to which that person is entitled under the provisions of an employee benefit plan, or for the purpose of interfering with the attainment of any right to which such participant may become entitled under the plan.

# FAMILY AND MEDICAL LEAVE ACT

The Family and Medical Leave Act of 1993 (FMLA) provides to eligible employees of covered employers up to 12 weeks of unpaid leave in each leave year for

- childbirth, adoption or foster placement;
- the serious medical condition of a spouse, child or parent (not including in-laws);
- the serious medical condition of the employee rendering the employee unable to perform the functions of his/her job.

Covered employers are those with 50 or more employees during each of 20 workweeks during the current or preceding calendar year. Eligible employees are those who have worked at least 12 months and at least 1,250 hours during the 12 months preceding FMLA leave commencement and work at worksites where 50 or more employees work within a 75-mile radius. An employee seeking FMLA leave must give the employer 30 days' notice if the leave is foreseeable (e.g., childbirth) or such lesser notice as is practicable. The employer may request medical certification of the reasons for leave (except childbirth) by a qualified health care provider. If the employer disbelieves the certification, the employer can utilize a challenge procedure permitting second and third certifications to resolve the issue.

While FMLA leave is unpaid, under certain circumstances employees may elect and employers may require that employees apply accrued paid vacation, personal, medical/sick and family leave during the FMLA leave period. In this sense, FMLA leave overlaps and runs concurrently with other forms of leave under existing leave plans. During FMLA leave, the employer must continue to provide health care benefits, but the provision of other benefits is not required. Upon return from FMLA leave, the employee must be restored to the same or an equivalent position, and all prior accrued benefits must be restored. To take credit against an employee's 12-week FMLA leave quota, the employer must designate leave as FMLA-qualifying prior to the employee's return from leave. The leave designation must advise the employee of eight specific rights and obligations under FMLA. Records of such designation notices should be maintained.

# LABOR UNION ISSUES

The National Labor Rights Act (NLRA) regulates relations between private sector employees and unions. The Wagner Act of 1935 ensured three fundamental employee rights: (1) the right to organize, (2) the right to collectively bargain and (3) the right to engage in concerted activities such as strikes and picketing. To guarantee these rights, the Wagner Act outlaws a variety of employer practices that interfere with union activity, including refusing to bargain with a union chosen by a majority of employees as their exclusive representative. To strengthen the bargaining process itself, a provision was added to require employers and unions to adhere to collective bargaining agreements during their term. Employee rights were strengthened by ensuring that employees could refrain from engaging in union or other concerted activities and by granting individual employees the right to discuss grievances directly with an employer. Provisions added in 1959 established special procedures to facilitate collective bargaining in the health care field and to require advance notice of strikes or picketing against health care institutions. Although this is an increasing issue in larger health care entities, unionization has not been a major issue in ASCs. Should any issues regarding unionization of employees arise, legal counsel should be consulted promptly as significant penalties could be assessed for violations of this act.

## GARNISHING WAGES

The Consumer Credit Protection Act (CCPA) prohibits employers from discharging an employee because his or her earnings have been subject to garnishment for any one debt, regardless of the number of levies made or proceedings brought to collect it. It does not, however, protect an employee from discharge if the employee's earnings have been subject to garnishment for a second or subsequent debts. Wage garnishment is a legal procedure through which the earnings of an individual are required by court order to be withheld by an employer and provided to someone other than the employee for the payment of a debt.

The amount of earnings that may be garnished in any workweek or pay period is limited to 25% of *disposable earnings* or the amount by which disposable earnings are greater than 30 times the federal minimum hourly wage, whichever is less. Disposable earnings is the amount of earnings left after legally required deductions have been made for federal, state and local taxes, Social Security, unemployment insurance and state employee retirement systems. Deductions that are not required by law, e.g., union dues, health and life insurance, and charitable contributions, are not subtracted from gross earnings when calculating the amount of disposable earnings for garnishment purposes. This limit applies regardless of the number of garnishment orders received by an employer. In court orders for child support or alimony, up to 50% of an employee's disposable earnings can be gar-

**Protecting Your ASC: A Legal Handbook**                                    **45**

nished if the employee is supporting a spouse or child, and up to 60% for an employee who is not. An additional five percent may be garnished for support payments that are more than 12 weeks in arrears. Such garnishments are not subject to the restrictions noted above.

These garnishment restrictions do not apply to bankruptcy court orders and debts due for federal and state taxes. Nor are these restrictions applicable to voluntary wage assignments, i.e., situations in which workers voluntarily agree that their employers may turn over some specified amount of their earnings to a creditor or creditors.

Employers who willfully violate the prohibition against discharge provisions of the law may be prosecuted criminally and fined up to $1,000, imprisoned for up to one year, or both.

States may also have similar laws that should be consulted. The federal law provides that if a state wage garnishment law differs from the federal law, whichever law provides the employee the greatest protection applies.

# USE OF LIE DETECTORS OR POLYGRAPHS

The Employee Polygraph Protection Act (EPPA) prohibits most private employers from using lie detector tests either for pre-employment screening or during the course of employment. Employers are generally prohibited from requiring or requesting any employee or job applicant to take a lie detector test; they are also generally prohibited from discharging, disciplining or discriminating against an employee or job applicant for refusing to take a test or for exercising other rights under EPPA. Employers may not use or inquire about the results of a lie detector test or discharge or discriminate against an employee or job applicant on the basis of the results of a test.

Subject to restrictions, the act permits polygraph (a type of lie detector) tests to be administered to certain job applicants of pharmaceutical manufacturers, distributors and dispensers. Subject to restrictions, the act also permits polygraph testing of certain employees who are reasonably suspected of involvement in a workplace incident, such as theft or embezzlement that resulted in specific economic loss or injury to the employer. When polygraph examinations are permitted, they are subject to strict standards concerning the conduct of the test. Before a polygraph is used, legal counsel should be consulted. The law does not preempt any provision of any state or local law or any collective bargaining agreement that is more restrictive with respect to lie detector tests.

Employers violating the law may be subject to civil money penalties up to $10,000 per violation and may also be liable to the employee for restitution, including employment, reinstatement, promotion and payment of lost wages and benefits.

## CONCLUSION

As an employer, ASCs are subject to a multitude of diverse federal laws. For more information on federal requirements, see the small business handbook at www.dol.gov/dol/asp/public/programs/handbook/main.htm or request a copy by calling 202.693.6460. In addition, all states have at least some laws protecting employees that add to the requirements discussed above. Increasingly, local jurisdictions, counties and cities are enacting laws addressing the rights of employees, such as those requiring domestic partners to be given the same insurance coverage as spouses. Local Chambers of Commerce or state agencies may be a good source of general information on state and local requirements. The prudent ASC manager and owner will consult with an attorney or a human resources expert in addressing human resources issues.

**Protecting Your ASC: A Legal Handbook** 47

# CHAPTER 7

# Reporting Adverse Events

Many states require health care facilities to report adverse events. These laws vary with regard to every detail, including who must report, what must be reported and what happens with the reported information. For example, most laws require reports to be filed by hospitals, but some also require reporting by ASCs. The nature of adverse events that must be reported varies from death to any serious injury. Before an injury or death occurs, you should determine if your state requires ASCs to report adverse events and, if so, what the exact requirements are. Once you are familiar with the requirements, implement a procedure to make sure that if an event requiring a report occurs, the report is made promptly. If the reports are available to the public, you may also want to put in place a plan for handling any media inquiries that may result from such reports.

## ADVERSE EVENT REPORTING RELATED TO MEDICAL DEVICES

The Safe Medical Devices Act of 1990 requires health care facilities, including ASCs, to report suspected medical device–related deaths to both the Food and Drug Administration (FDA) and the manufacturer. *Medical device* is defined as any health care product that does not achieve any of its principal intended purposes by chemical action in or on the body or by being metabolized and therefore includes everything from thermometers and tongue depressors to pacemakers and kidney dialysis machines. Medical device–related serious injuries need be reported only to the manufacturer. If the medical device manufacturer is unknown, the facility reports the serious injury to the FDA. Reports must be made within 10 days of the ASC becoming aware of the information. Your ASC should have a process for making such reports. In addition, annual reports are

**Protecting Your ASC: A Legal Handbook**

required. Forms for reporting such adverse events can be obtained from the FDA by calling 301.827.0360 or from its web site at www.fda.gov.

## ADVERSE EVENT REPORTING RELATED TO DRUGS

Currently, no federal law requires user facilities such as ASCs to report adverse events related to drugs; however, the FDA encourages ASCs to use their voluntary reporting systems to report such incidents. Voluntary reports can be made by calling 1.800.FDA.1088, or reports can be made online at www.fda.gov. Of course, state adverse event reporting systems described above may require reporting of adverse events related to drugs.

## CONCLUSION

It is important to know the requirements your state has for reporting adverse events. In addition, you need to understand the requirements of the Safe Medical Devices Act and be familiar with the FDA's voluntary reporting system for adverse events involving drugs. Implement policies for handling such events before they occur.

# CHAPTER 8

# Taxation and Pension Planning Issues

ASCs increasingly must concern themselves with issues related to tax-exempt entities and a variety of other tax aspects of ventures. An ASC most often addresses tax exemption when it is formed as a joint venture between physicians and a tax-exempt hospital and/or health care system. If the ASC does not comply with regulations applicable to tax-exempt entities, then the tax-exempt entity may not be permitted to invest in the ASC or be a partner in the ASC without risking its tax-exempt status. This chapter discusses the IRS regulations that affect how a tax-exempt entity can structure its ownership and control of an ASC joint venture.

ASCs also must address various tax and pension planning issues. For example, ASC owners will be very displeased with the ASC if they are taxed on ASC income but not permitted to receive monies from the ASC to pay those taxes. Moreover, many physicians will have difficulty investing in the ASC and being partners in the ASC if doing so will impede their ability to fully operate their own tax-deferred pension plans. This chapter outlines some of the significant tax issues that arise in joint venture planning.

## STRUCTURING JOINT VENTURES BETWEEN TAX-EXEMPT ENTITIES AND PHYSICIANS

The application of IRS principles to a joint venture may give rise to conflict between physicians and tax-exempt hospital partners in forming and operating the venture. The hospital will often indicate to the physician partners that it cannot permit them to have a certain amount of control of the venture without the hospital risking its tax-exempt status. The physicians often believe that the hospital is hiding behind tax-exempt status to avoid making certain business arrangements that it simply does not want to make.

The source of the conflict is the IRS position that a tax-exempt entity can maintain its tax-exempt status only if its involvement in the venture is viewed as furthering its charitable purposes. Its involvement in the venture cannot be perceived as serving non-exempt purposes or serving private or individual benefits.

The applicable regulations specify the following:

(c) Operational test-(1) Primary activities. An organization will be regarded as operated exclusively for one or more exempt purposes only if it engages primarily in activities which accomplish one or more of such exempt purposes specified in section 501(c)(3). An organization will not be so regarded if more than an insubstantial part of its activities is not in furtherance of an exempt purpose.[8]

The operational test focuses on the actual purposes that the organization serves rather than its statement of purpose. Consistent with this concept, a tax-exempt entity's participation in a joint venture must also serve these organizational and operational mandates.

Whether participation in an ASC joint venture will constitute engaging primarily in activities that accomplish an exempt purpose is a question of fact to be resolved based on all the evidence presented relating to the venture. The burden of proof is on the tax-exempt entity to demonstrate that involvement in the ASC is consistent with its mission to be operated exclusively for tax-exempt purposes and that it does not benefit private interests more than incidentally.

IRS exemption decisions have generally included the promotion of health for the benefit of the community as a whole as a part of the definition of charitable purposes, which are considered exempt under the operational test. Promotion of health for the benefit of the community as a whole, however, means not only providing a health care service but also employing a standard that reflects a policy of ensuring that adequate health care services are actually *delivered* to those in the community who need them. Under this standard, health care providers must meet a flexible community benefit test based upon a variety of factors.

An organization is deemed not to operate exclusively for tax-exempt purposes if it operates for the benefit of private interests such as physicians, organization shareholders or persons controlled, directly or indirectly, by such private interests. The mere fact that an exempt organization enters into a partnership agreement with private parties that receive returns on their capital investments does not establish that the organization has impermissibly conferred private benefits or failed to serve exempt purposes. Rather, the venture is judged by whether the participation will further the

52          Chapter 8 • Taxation and Pension Planning Issues

exempt entity's charitable purposes and whether the venture will improperly serve private interests.

The IRS provided some guidance on its interpretation of these regulations when it issued Revenue Ruling 98-15, in which it employed a facts-and-circumstances approach to determine whether a hospital could participate in a whole hospital joint venture with for-profit entities without jeopardizing its tax-exempt status. Although Revenue Ruling 98-15 clearly evidenced the IRS's concern about the charitable status of tax-exempt entities that participate in joint ventures with for-profit entities, it did not directly address ancillary joint ventures, such as a tax-exempt hospital's ownership of an interest in an ASC.

A year later, however, the Tax Court issued a decision in *Redlands Surgical Services v. Commissioner*[9] on an ancillary joint venture between a charitable hospital, a for-profit enterprise and physician partners. Redlands Health Services (RHS) Corporation was the sole owner of Redlands Community Hospital. Both were tax exempt under federal tax laws. RHS also was the sole member of Redlands Surgical Services (RSS), which sought tax-exempt status as well. RSS formed a partnership with Redlands–SCA Surgery Centers, Inc. (SCA), a for-profit entity. That partnership, named Redlands Ambulatory Surgery Center Partnership (RASC), served as the general partner of Inland Surgery Center Limited Partnership (ISC) and had 32 physician limited partners. RASC was managed by a committee consisting of four managing directors, two chosen by RSS and two chosen by SCA. Day-to-day management of the ASC was provided by SCA Management, Inc., an entity that was wholly owned by the same corporation that owned SCA.

RSS's application for tax-exempt status was denied by the IRS based in part upon its conclusion that RSS did not have real control over the assets or activities of RSC or ISC. The IRS asserted that the operation of ISC did not benefit a broad cross section of the community and conferred substantial private benefit on the for-profit owners. The IRS also believed that the 25-year term of the management contract with a for-profit entity was unreasonably long and difficult to terminate.

Upon appeal, the Tax Court agreed that RSS had ceded effective control over the operations of the partnerships and the ASC to private parties, thereby conferring an impermissible private benefit. The court further noted that none of the contracts involved—the RASC General Partnership Agreement, the ISC Limited Partnership Agreement and the management contract with SCA—required operations to be guided by any charitable or community benefit, goal, policy or objective. The court found no other

**Protecting Your ASC: A Legal Handbook**　　　　　　　　　　　　　　　　**53**

evidence of an obligation that charitable purposes be placed ahead of economic objectives in the ASC's operations. It also noted that a quality assurance agreement between the hospital and ISC had been terminated, which it believed called into question the tax-exempt entity's ability to provide enough services to meet patient needs. Additionally, noting the non-competition provisions of the RASC General Partnership Agreement, the court concluded that RSS had restricted its own ability to assess and serve community needs for outpatient services. The decision of the Tax Court was upheld in a one-paragraph ruling by the Ninth Circuit Court of Appeals issued on March 15, 2001.[10]

In light of Revenue Ruling 98-15, the *Redlands* decision and other IRS pronouncements and interpretations in this arena, some practical suggestions and concepts that can be employed in establishing joint ventures with tax-exempt entities follow.

### NEW PROVIDER

As a general rule, a venture that creates a new provider or clearly improves services, equipment or technology will be easier to defend as serving the community than a venture that is simply built out of an existing service provider.

### RESERVE POWERS

In forming the joint-venture, the tax-exempt entity should reserve sufficient powers to ensure that the ASC serves tax-exempt purposes. Those reserve powers relate to such items as the ASC's budget (operating and capital), the selection of key executives, the amount of community care to be provided by the ASC, the closing of staff privileges for the ASC and the development of intraparty relationships with the ASC.

### BOARD PROPORTION

Representation on the board of the joint venture should generally be proportionate to ownership in the venture.

### OWNERSHIP OF VENTURE

The tax-exempt entity typically should own at least 30% (and usually more) of the entity. This helps to clarify that the venture is not intended to provide private benefits, but is intended and is required to provide community benefits.

### PROPORTIONATE GUARANTEES

Guarantees for debt and other obligations of the entity should be pro rata by the parties. The tax-exempt entity generally should not disproportionately guarantee debt for the joint venture entity.

### SUFFICIENT CAPITALIZATION

The venture should have what is best characterized as "normal" capitalization. The tax-exempt entity should not provide all assets for the entity. Otherwise, the venture could be perceived as a shell by which to share profits without significant capital expenditure or investment.

### STATEMENT OF COMMUNITY BENEFITS AND PURPOSES

The governing documents for the venture should clearly indicate the community benefits and purposes that are to be served by the venture.

### COMMUNITY BENEFITS TRUMP PROFITS

The governing documents should clarify that the priority for the venture is to provide community benefits over maximizing profits. Here, again, the venture may provide for either a qualified or a categorical trumping of profit by community purposes.

### PERIODIC REVIEW: CATALOG BENEFITS

The venture should periodically review community benefits provided; it should also aim to catalog the benefits the venture offers. This is particularly true if the venture evolves out of an existing business.

### DEVELOP AND BROADCAST POLICY

The venture should develop a charitable core and indigent pay policy. It should also broadcast its policy to serve all patients regardless of their ability to pay.

### COMPLIANCE WITH INTERNAL REVENUE CODE SECTION 4958

The tax-exempt entity should follow the process established in IRS regulations that enables it to demonstrate that payment relationships between the tax-exempt entity and the ASC or the ASC's affiliates are proper. A presumption that a transaction is proper may be established under the regulations by satisfying the following three requirements: (1) the compensation arrangement or terms of transfer must be approved by the organization's governing body or a committee of the governing body, composed entirely of individuals who do not have a conflict of interest with respect to the arrangement or transaction; (2) the governing body, or committee, must obtain and rely upon appropriate data as to comparability prior to

**Protecting Your ASC: A Legal Handbook**

making its determination; and (3) the governing body or committee must adequately document the basis for its determination concurrently with making that determination. The presumption established by satisfying these three requirements may be rebutted by additional information showing that the compensation was not reasonable or that the transfer was not at fair market value.

The governing body of the tax-exempt entity should obtain and review an independent and contemporaneous valuation if the transaction involves any transfer of assets or business between the parties, or if there are other financial relationships between the parties to the venture. It is important that the valuations be provided contemporaneously so that the parties are not viewed as manufacturing the valuations after the fact to help ratify the transaction.

For the purposes of Internal Revenue Code Section 4958, appropriate data include, but are not limited to, compensation levels paid by similarly situated organizations, both taxable and tax-exempt, for functionally comparable positions; the availability of similar services in the geographic area of the applicable tax-exempt organization; independent compensation surveys compiled by independent firms; actual written offers from similar institutions competing for the services of the party that could be seen as having a conflict of interest; and independent appraisals of the value of property that the applicable tax-exempt organization intends to purchase from, or sell or provide to, the party as to whom there could be a conflict of interest.

The transaction's approval must be documented properly. The written or electronic records of the governing body or committee must note the terms of the transaction that were approved, the date on which the transaction was approved, the members of the governing body or committee who were present during debate on the transaction or arrangement, those who voted on it, the data obtained and relied upon by the committee in its consideration of the transaction, the source of these data and the actions taken with respect to consideration of the transaction by anyone who otherwise is a member of the governing body or committee but who had a conflict of interest with respect to the transaction. If the governing body or committee determines that reasonable compensation for a specific arrangement is higher or lower than the range of comparable data obtained, the governing body or committee must record the basis for its determination. For a decision to be documented concurrently, records must be prepared by the next meeting of the governing body or committee occurring after the final action or actions of the governing body or committee are taken. Records must be reviewed and approved by the governing body or committee as reasonable, accurate and complete within a reasonable time period thereafter.

Finally, the threat to the tax-exempt status of a charitable organization that wishes to joint venture with for-profit entities in an ASC enterprise can be avoided if the charitable organization creates a for-profit subsidiary to act as the partner in the joint venture as long as the following factors are present:

- the for-profit subsidiary is not funded with tax-exempt financing
- there is no private inurement from the tax-exempt entity (e.g., the tax-exempt entity does not contribute assets or provide services for reimbursement for less than fair market value)
- the for-profit subsidiary is operated separately from the tax-exempt entity (e.g., separate boards of directors, management and financial records)
- the for-profit entity has distinct purposes
- the day-to-day operations of the for-profit entity and the tax-exempt entity are separate

These characteristics will not assist the tax-exempt entity if the subsidiary engages in illegal activities but should help prevent exposure where the subsidiary simply does not have enough control to ensure that community purposes are being served by the ASC joint venture.

# CASH VS. ACCRUAL ACCOUNTING
# FOR TAX PURPOSES

Given the choice, many ASCs would use the cash basis of accounting for calculating income tax. This method delays the payment of income taxes on income that may have accrued but for which payments have not actually been received.

The Internal Revenue Code limits the extent to which the cash method can be used by ASCs. Specifically, Section 448(a) of the code provides that the cash method may not be used by (a) a C corporation, (b) a partnership that has a C corporation as a partner or (c) a tax shelter. The limitations provided for C corporations and partnerships with C corporation partners are not applicable, however, to entities with annual gross receipts of less than $5 million, so the majority of ASCs that are structured as corporations or partnerships are not precluded from using the cash method. On

**Protecting Your ASC: A Legal Handbook**                                                   **57**

the other hand, the definition of *tax shelter* is fairly broad and can apply to many ASCs, thereby requiring them nevertheless to use the accrual method. Tax shelters under Section 461(i) of the code include (x) any enterprise if at any time interests in such enterprise have been offered for sale in any offering required to be registered under any federal or state agency having the authority to regulate the offering of securities for sale; (y) any syndicate within the meaning of section 1256(e)(3)(B) of the code; and (z) any tax shelter as defined in section 6662(d)(2)(C)(ii) of the code. The syndicate rules were not drafted to be applicable to ASCs; nevertheless, they state that an entity shall be deemed a syndicate if more than 35% of its interests are held by limited partners or limited entrepreneurs. This statement may be interpreted to preclude use of the cash basis of accounting for limited partnerships and limited liability corporations in which greater than 35% of the ownership is held by non-managing physicians. Furthermore, some commentators have asserted that the provision that qualifies an enterprise as a tax shelter because of securities registration might be interpreted to cover entities that are merely required to file materials with the state and federal government to perfect a securities exemption, such as a Form D filing for a Regulation D private placement.

## PENSION PLANS - AFFILIATED SERVICES GROUP ISSUES

The *affiliated services group* sections of the tax code may present problems for some ASCs. A broad interpretation of the pension plan rules of Section 414(M)(2)(A) could lead to the conclusion that a physician who owns interests in an ASC and performs services at the ASC should be required to treat the ASC and the physician's private medical practice as affiliated entities. If so, those entities could be treated as a single employer for purposes of determining whether a physician's qualified retirement plan met certain minimum participation requirements of the IRS. If not, the plan could be disqualified. The argument arises because of code sections that provide that two parties are deemed affiliated if the first organization is a service organization that is a shareholder or a partner in a second organization and either performs services for the second organization or is regularly associated with the second organization in providing services to third parties. Proposed regulations under these sections indicate that the intent is to ensure that organizations providing services hand-in-hand are treated as affiliated for employee benefit plan testing purposes. Examples include situations in which law partners share offices and jointly provide

58　　　　　Chapter 8 • Taxation and Pension Planning Issues

services to third parties, or in which physicians or others act in concert with similar employees to provide services. Other examples focus on the joint ownership of management services organizations. Although the ASC and its physician partners might technically be viewed as associated in providing services to third parties, this result does not appear to have been intended by the drafters of these sections of the code. Nevertheless, administrators and lawyers representing ASCs should be aware of this possible interpretation and seek legal advice to avoid potential problems.

## CONCLUSION

In general, the tax issues for ASCs are similar to those confronted by other businesses. With the exception of the three issues discussed in this chapter, following general tax advice should create no problems. However, should you consider a joint venture between a for-profit and not-for-profit entity, you should proceed carefully.

# CHAPTER 9

# ASC Sales and Acquisitions

At some point, the issue of whether or not to pursue a sale of your ASC may arise. Whether it arises because a potential buyer approaches you or you want to seek a buyer, you should be aware of some basics to consider as you move forward.

National proprietary chains own interests in a significant percentage of the country's ASCs. These companies may own only ASCs or may also own hospitals and physician practices. In most situations, such companies own ASCs as joint ventures with doctors and provide substantial services to assist the ASC in its daily operations. Usually these companies acquire interests in already established ASCs, so your ASC may receive an offer to purchase an interest. On the other hand, if you are interested, you can pursue such an offer.

Each company evaluates potential acquisitions using its own criteria and pursues different strategies for completing acquisitions. For example, a company may target ASCs in areas where the acquisition will complement its hospital operations and its development of a managed care strategy regardless of whether the ASC is multi-specialty or financially sound on its own. Another company may own ASCs as a complement to physician practice management. Other companies may target extremely robust single-specialty ASCs. For companies that do not have hospital or physician operations, the ASC must stand on its own as a profitable venture. Therefore, such companies generally search more selectively for robust multi-specialty ASCs.

Regardless of how the discussion arises, there are several factors that should be considered. This chapter provides a general overview; the exact details of your transaction will depend upon factors such as ownership structure of the ASC, state law, the ASC's assets and the potential buyers.

**Protecting Your ASC: A Legal Handbook**                                              **61**

# Overview of Sales Process

A sales transaction, whether with a company, a group of doctors or an individual, typically involves a number of steps. These include the following:

1. Enter into confidentiality agreement with potential buyers.
2. Assemble information regarding the ASC to provide to buyers.
3. Set internal goals as to critical issues—ownership post-transaction, purchase price, etc.
4. Package and provide information to potential buyers.
5. Conduct due diligence regarding the potential buyers.
6. Set up site visits and negotiation visits with potential buyers.
7. Review state CON and license issues to ascertain requirements relating to transfers of ownership.
8. Negotiate and sign letter of intent with selected buyer.
9. Negotiate acquisition agreements and new partnership agreements.
10. Make all necessary state CON and licensure filings.
11. Buyer conducts and completes its due diligence.
12. Coordinate closing to coincide with state approval periods, ASC approval meetings (board and shareholder) and close transactions.
13. Obtain new licenses and provider numbers.

## Questions to ASC Potential Partners/Buyers

If, as is often the case, existing owners of the ASC will enter a joint venture with the buyers following the sale, evaluating the potential joint venture partners in a variety of ways is critical to ensuring a good fit after the sale. Questions that administrators, boards, owners and others should examine in determining which company to joint venture with include the following:

- Does the company have a track record of joint venturing with physicians?
- What purchase price will the joint venture pay for the ASC assets?
- How will control be shared once the joint venture is established?
- Does the ASC company have a history of success and of paying distributions to ASC partners?
- Are physicians in other ventures pleased to have the company as a partner?
- Does the company have a record of legal compliance?

- What percentage of the joint venture does the company want?
- Will the management agreement with the company limit the company's ability to use ASC funds to pay for the company's central overhead?
- Does the company have the funds with which to complete the acquisition?
- What will the company charge for management services?
- What commitment will the management company make to being on-site when needed?
- Does the company have sufficient resources locally to assist in management?
- Does the company have any particular managed care contracting strength or record?
- Does the company have arrangements that will allow the ASC to achieve cost savings, such as purchasing discounts?
- Is the company's philosophy consistent with the philosophy of the existing owners and managers?

## ISSUES TO RESOLVE IN NEGOTIATIONS

The types of issues that will need to be addressed include the following:

- ownership percentage
- valuation and purchase price
- management and lease relationships
- board control
- non-competition covenants
- indemnity responsibilities
- tax consequences of the sale

As you prepare for the process, you should begin considering the issues. In addition to the operational issues, several legal issues, including the following, may need to be resolved for the acquisition to go forward:

- fraud and abuse compliance
- tax-exempt requirements, if applicable
- state CON requirements, if applicable
- state licensure
- Medicare transfer rules

**Protecting Your ASC: A Legal Handbook**

## VALUATION ISSUES

This section provides a brief overview of transaction-related valuation issues. There are three distinct methods for valuing ASCs: market, replacement or cost, and discounted cash flow. Because of both legal and financing concerns, many ASC transactions cannot be completed without a third-party valuation. For example, a hospital board may need an independent valuation to buy into a physician-owned ASC or to sell interests in an ASC it owns so that it can demonstrate that it is paying or receiving fair market value for its interests. Similarly, a lender may require a valuation prior to providing financing to an existing or proposed ASC. While formal valuations are critical, parties can use certain rules of thumb to gain an understanding of potential valuation. The following is a brief discussion of those rules of thumb.

### MARKET

Typically the purchasing company will value the ASC at some multiple of net income. A variation is to apply the multiple to EBITDA (earnings before interest, taxes, depreciation and amortization) rather than net income. Obviously, the same multiple applied to EBITDA will result in a higher number than if applied to net income. The multiple is based on the ASC's likelihood of success. Of course, the key to a proper and reasonable valuation is selecting a multiple that properly values the ASC. Factors that can lead to higher multiples being applied and thus a higher valuation of the ASC include the following:

- reliance on many staff physicians
- CON limits on competition
- reliance on specialties with increasing reimbursement (e.g., orthopedics; ear, nose and throat)
- limited competition
- efficiencies and economies of scale in certain specialties—full use of expensive equipment by multiple surgeons
- numerous owners
- multiple payers in the market without the dominance of one or two payers
- limited price or reimbursement pressure
- reasonable cost structure (labor, facility, etc.)

Factors leading to lower multiples, in contrast, include the following:

- extensive and aggressive payer discounting

- primary care market control
- hospital price competition
- managed care control and steering to other providers
- heavy reliance on one or two doctors
- excessive debt or cost burden
- heavy reliance on one or two specialties
- strong reliance on lower reimbursement procedures
- inability to manage costs

### REPLACEMENT OR COST METHOD

The cost or replacement method of valuing an ASC does not take into account cash flows. Rather, it solely accounts for the actual cost to replace the assets that are being purchased. Thus, a party valuing an ASC on a cost or replacement value basis would examine the cost to replace the tenant improvements, the equipment, the working capital and the other inventory type assets that are available. Because this method disregards the actual business generated by the ASC, an important asset in many situations, this approach has limited applicability in most situations.

### DISCOUNTED CASH FLOW METHOD

A discounted cash flow method of valuation is the one preferred by the IRS. Earnings of the ASC are estimated for the next five years. A reversionary or terminal value is also placed on the ASC. These estimates are generated by analyzing such items as revenues per procedure, total revenues, expenses, the need to reinvest money in the business and a variety of other factors that affect cash flow. The estimated cash flow amounts for years one to five and their terminal value are then discounted back to a present value. The discount rate takes into account the level of risk related to the ASC. A higher discount rate means a lower present value. In essence, a higher discount rate would reflect a higher risk ASC. Changes in the assumptions related to cash flow can greatly affect the valuation of the ASC.

# POTENTIAL VIOLATIONS OF THE ANTI-KICKBACK LAW

Transactions involving ASCs can raise numerous issues under the federal anti-kickback statute. A brief discussion of relevant issues follows.

**Protecting Your ASC: A Legal Handbook**

## PURCHASE PRICE

The purchase price paid for an ASC generally exceeds the fair market value of the tangible or hard assets. This fact has led authorities to question whether or not the portion of purchase price that is for intangible items is actually a payment to induce the physician seller to continue to refer patients to the entity after the sale is completed. The OIG noted in a letter to the IRS that it would or could attack an acquisition based on the amount of the purchase price allocated to intangible assets (i.e., goodwill, patient records and lists, and covenant not to compete). It has not, however, done so.

## PAYING FOR ASC WITH STOCK OR NOTES

Again, the issue raised is, does the payment of purchase price in the form of stock or notes induce referrals to the entity after the sale? The severity of the risk depends upon the justification for providing stock or notes and the impact that referrals from the physician are likely to have on the stock price or the buyer's ability to make payments under the notes. For example, if the buyer can adequately set forth reasons for payment in notes or stock that are wholly unrelated to referrals, then payment, in that form, should be defensible. Such reasons may include that the cost of paying through notes or stock, rather than cash, is lower to the buyer due to cost of obtaining capital. The greater impact that referrals from the selling physician are likely to have on the sale price or the buyer's ability to make payments on a note, the greater the risk. Accordingly, stock in a large, publicly traded company poses little problem, as any referrals the physician would make would have virtually no impact on the stock. However, if the value of the stock exceeds the value of the ASC, the same problems would exist as with cash of the equivalent amount. Moreover, if the buyer designates who will own post-transaction stock or ASC interests based on who can generate more or less business for the ASC, the transaction is problematic.

## REFERRALS TO OTHER ENTITIES BUYER OWNS

In many acquisition transactions, the selling physicians have the ability to provide referrals to both the business being sold and related businesses operated by the purchaser. For example, an acquirer of an ASC may also operate a hospital lab or a physical therapy operation that accepts referrals from the selling physicians and/or the ASC. To the extent that these facts exist, it is critical that the buyer and seller be able to demonstrate that the transaction was not effected with the intent, expressed or implied, to generate referrals for these other services. Demonstrating a benign intent depends upon factors present when the transaction takes place and upon evidence developed over the years following the transaction. For example, at the time of the transaction, it is critical that the financial projections and deliberations of the acquiring company not reflect an attempt to "buy" physician referrals for ancillary services. Moreover, it is critical that the profitability of the transaction stand on its own and in no way be evaluated with regard to the economic synergy between the acquiring entity and its related services.

With respect to post-transaction actions, it is critical that the acquiring party (1) not structure ongoing relationships with the sellers in a way that encourages the provision of referrals to ancillary services, (2) not encourage the usage of ancillary services by the selling physicians (e.g., moving of ancillary service offices to locales near the doctors or providing of physician access to the purchaser's sales representatives), and (3) not take any explicit action after closing that would alter the perception of the deal from a third party's perspective (e.g., if a hospital that acquired a physician-owned ASC immediately took steps to close the ASC, it would become apparent that a purpose of the transaction was to steer the procedures to the hospital rather than to the acquired ASC).

## POST-TRANSACTION EMPLOYMENT OR MANAGEMENT RELATIONSHIPS

Concurrently with the transaction, the purchaser may enter into a management agreement with the selling company. To the extent that the payment for management services exceeds fair market value for the services rendered, it is likely that the relationship will be viewed as intended to cause referrals. Accordingly, it is important that the parties, through both appraisal and documentation of efforts, be able to substantiate that the compensation provided is at fair market value. Moreover, it is critical that compensation be set in such a manner that does not reward or punish a party for referrals or lack thereof.

**Protecting Your ASC: A Legal Handbook**      **67**

## POST-TRANSACTION SALE OF STOCK

It is common for the acquiring company to acquire the assets of the ASC, then sell interests in the new company to existing physician holders or to new physicians who can generate referrals to the ASC. To the extent that the physicians are selected to purchase more or less stock based on the volume or value of potential referrals or because they are in a position to make referrals to the ASC, it is possible that an anti-kickback charge could be made, depending on how the ASC is structured. Such individuals' ability to buy into the ASC at lower per-unit prices than were paid by the acquiring company also raises issues. To defend such a practice, it is critical that the transaction structure comply with the ASC safe harbor or the small investment interest safe harbor to the extent feasible. In this regard, it is highly recommended that an appraisal be obtained that clarifies that the physicians acquiring units are paying fair market value for the units. See discussion of these issues in chapter 11.

# TAXATION ISSUES

Income tax consequences can vary significantly depending on how the transaction is structured. Although a detailed presentation of tax issues is beyond the scope of this document, it is important to understand certain basic considerations.

Most ASC transactions are structured either as sales of assets or as sales of the stock held by the owners of the ASC. In an asset sale, the entity owning the ASC is taxed on the gain or loss recognized on each asset being sold, taking into account the seller's basis in the asset and the amount by which an allocated portion of the overall purchase price exceeds that basis. If the selling entity then liquidates, the proceeds of the sale may be taxed again at the shareholder level when they are distributed to the entity's owners.

The purchaser of the assets receives a basis equal to the fair market value of the assets. This typically results in a higher basis in the assets for the purchaser than the old basis was for the seller. The excess of the purchase price over fair market value of the assets may result in good will, which is tax-deductible over time.

Because a stock transaction occurs directly between the purchaser and the owner of the ASC entity, there is no tax at the ASC entity level. The selling shareholders are taxed on their capital gains from the sale, which represent the excess of the purchase price over the tax basis of the stock sold. In a stock acquisition, the purchaser's tax basis in the stock is the amount paid for it. Unlike the asset acquisition, the purchaser generally does not have the opportunity to "step-up" the basis in the assets being acquired.

There are many factors that can alter the results identified above, including whether the seller is a C corporation or an S corporation and whether the purchaser wishes to avail itself of the opportunity presented by the Internal Revenue Code to treat a stock transaction as a *deemed asset sale*. Acquisitions also can be accomplished through various forms of mergers and combinations, which have their own rules and consequences. Because the tax structure of an acquisition can significantly affect the ultimate financial impact of the transaction on both the purchaser and the seller, it is important to work with a competent tax advisor to assure that your objectives are met.

## CONCLUSION

Whether you come to the issue of a sale as a purchaser or a seller, many factors must be considered. This chapter provided an overview of some of the key issues you must consider as you begin the discussions of your sales transaction.

**Protecting Your ASC: A Legal Handbook**

# CHAPTER 10

# Antitrust Considerations

The antitrust laws can either be helpful or harmful to an ASC depending on the specific circumstances. For example, ASCs are increasingly concerned about exclusive contracting between hospitals and payers and, in certain instances, with physicians. In these types of situations, the antitrust laws can be helpful to ASCs. If the ASC can demonstrate that a hospital is engaged in conduct that violates the antitrust laws, the exclusive arrangement can be overturned.

On the other hand, a hospital may be able to claim an antitrust violation in situations where the great majority of the physicians that use an ASC are owners of the ASC by arguing that the ASC is attempting to control the market for certain types of outpatient surgical services. Problems may also arise where a hospital and an ASC—through a joint venture or otherwise—contract jointly with managed care payers, thus possibly excluding other ASCs from the market. In joint venture situations, there is an increasing likelihood that either the federal government or health care plans will bring action alleging that the combination of efforts by the ASC and its joint venture partner (in many cases a hospital) has the effect of fixing prices; similarly, mergers or combinations of ASCs and hospital providers may be attacked as attempting to monopolize the market for services.

Two federal antitrust statutes primarily affect ASCs. The Sherman Act prohibits collaborative actions such as group boycotts and price fixing and other restraints of trade. For example, an ASC cannot jointly develop with other ASCs a fee schedule or refuse to participate in an insurer's plan because prices or other conditions are unacceptable. The second federal statute, the Clayton Act, prohibits mergers when "the effect of such acquisition may be substantially to lessen competition, or to tend to create a monopoly." Antitrust actions may be brought by the government or by private parties allegedly injured by the antitrust violation.

**Protecting Your ASC: A Legal Handbook**                                         **71**

Clayton Act issues are most likely to be raised in the context of joint venture or mergers or combinations in smaller market areas. To show monopoly under the Clayton Act, it must be demonstrated that there is a reasonable probability that the proposed merger would substantially lessen competition. The Clayton Act prohibition was explained by one court as forbidding "mergers that are likely to hurt consumers, as by making it easier for the firms in the market to collude, expressly or tacitly, and thereby force price above or farther above the competitive level."[11] In analyzing potential Clayton Act issues, one looks at the post-acquisition market share.

To determine whether or not there is a reasonable probability of a substantial lessening of competition, the courts have focused on whether or not the proposed transaction has the "potential for creating, enhancing, or facilitating the exercise of market power—the ability of one or more firms to raise prices above competitive levels for a significant period of time."[12] Generally, a Clayton Act case may be established by demonstrating that the merged or joint venture entity will have a large or dominant percentage of the *relevant market* so that the entity can may raise prices above competitive levels.

A relevant market consists of two components: a product market and a geographic market. A properly defined product market includes any potential supplier who can readily offer consumers an alternative to the defendants' services (i.e., a hospital outpatient department is an alternative to an ASC). The market may exclude those potential suppliers whose product is sufficiently different. The geographic market can be defined by distance or time but generally will be analyzed using data on where patients that visit the different health care entities in question reside.

Whether brought under the Sherman or Clayton Act, a number of issues are commonly litigated under the antitrust laws in health care cases. These include issues such as whether the market power obtained by an ASC or the hospital has been obtained through a natural or non-natural monopoly, whether or not the hospital (i.e., a municipal hospital) is immune from prosecution under the antitrust laws as an agent of the state, whether or not the hospital and physicians are involved in price fixing, and whether or not certain parties are involved in group boycott or other anticompetitive actions. The following sections provide an overview of some of the issues that can affect ASCs under the antitrust laws. Most states have laws similar to these federal statutes.

# NATURAL VS. NON-NATURAL MONOPOLIES

When an ASC or other entity grows naturally to acquire a high per-centage of cases in a specialty, a so-called natural monopoly is created. This can be fully lawful. It could be illegal, in contrast, if the purpose of growth in a specialty is intended to keep out other competitors. For example, in a physician case, a court found no antitrust violation even though the physician group had a 100% market share in urology because the market share had developed naturally. A quote from this case demonstrates why the court found this arrangement acceptable:

> Starting with urology, which displays a 100% postmerger market share, the evidence shows that the entire market is comprised of only two urologists, Drs. Fagan and Humble. (Exhibit PX-454.) After the merger, both urologists plan to practice together at the River Region Clinic. Although Columbia urges this Court to find the merger presumptively unlawful on the basis of this 100% postmerger market share in urology, the evidence contains practical, common-sense reasons that justify a combined practice between these two doctors. According to the testimony of physician witnesses, the key issue for doctors is back-up or physician coverage. . . . Considering the specific charac-ter of this two-person market that exists within a relatively small medical community, this Court finds it inconceivable that Congress intended the Clayton Act to prohibit two urologists in Vicksburg, Mississippi from practicing together under the same roof. The practical effect of such an impractical statutory interpretation could be to deprive two physicians from taking alternate weekends off or an occasional family vacation. With the real-life implications of this alleged antitrust violation in mind, it appears to this Court that, if there is any arguable monopoly here at all, it is a "natural monop-oly." . . . If an entire county has only 12 physicians, one can hardly expect or want them to set up in competition with each other. We live in the age of technology and specialization in medical services. Physicians practice in groups, in alliances, in net-works, utilizing expensive equipment and support. Twelve physicians competing in a county would be competing to provide horse-and-buggy medicine.[13]

# PRICE FIXING

When an ASC and a hospital venture partner jointly contract with pay-ers, this can (under certain circumstances) expose the parties to liability as two parties acting jointly to fix prices. This risk is greatest when the hospi-tal owns less than 80% to 90% of the ASC. In this situation the court may view the hospital as a competitor and thus a separate party under the antitrust laws. By acting in unity, they may be illegally fixing prices.

Price-fixing allegations can also arise when two or more ASCs are inde-pendent of each other and discuss fee schedules or other pricing terms. Price fixing occurs or arises when parties agree expressly or implicitly to keep their prices at the same rate and not to compete based on price. Antitrust cases are extremely costly to defend, and thus it is good to avoid

Protecting Your ASC: A Legal Handbook   73

situations that might raise concerns. Usually, the comparison of fees with an ASC that is outside of one's own market area leads to little risk.

## STATE ACTION AND PETITIONING TO GOVERNMENT IMMUNITIES

Hospitals or other health care entities accused of violating antitrust laws by ASCs may defend their actions by claiming immunity using one of two theories relating to governmental action—*state action* or *petitioning the government*. If either is applicable it will be a complete defense. Based upon the principle that the states are sovereign, the courts have provided immunity or an exception to the antitrust laws known as the state action. Under this exception, if actions can be defined to be state action, there is no antitrust violation. This immunity was originally necessary to protect actions of utilities (such as electrical companies) that had been given monopolies by the state. Hospitals operating under state charters may claim this immunity. However, courts often construe this immunity narrowly so that it is only available where the state has clearly intended to provide such immunity. For example, one Louisiana ASC defeated a hospital's claim of state action immunity.[14]

Another antitrust exception protects efforts to secure government action. Based upon our right to petition our government, the US Supreme Court has held that antitrust liability cannot be predicated solely on petitioning to secure government action. For example, a hospital or ASC may take action to prevent a potential competitor from obtaining a CON. In general, such conduct is immune from antitrust laws. Similarly, ASCs can join to influence state or federal regulatory requirements. However, one must use care because if any other actions are taken together with petitioning the government, a potential conspiracy may be alleged to exist.

## GROUP BOYCOTT

Hospitals increasingly are taking action to try to exclude ASCs from insurance panels. Where hospitals act together to try to exclude an ASC or cause an insurer to boycott an ASC, this can be viewed as violating the antitrust laws.

# CONCLUSION

An ASC may use antitrust laws to deflect competition from hospitals. On the other hand, a hospital may claim that an ASC has violated antitrust laws when a majority of physicians that use the ASC are owners of the ASC. In joint ventures, an ASC must make certain that the ASC can defend itself against any charges that it is trying to fix prices. Similarly, in mergers or combinations of ASCs and hospital providers, you must be prepared to counter charges of monopolizing the market.

Antitrust cases are extremely complicated, lengthy, costly and difficult to win. Accordingly, few ASCs will be able to obtain relief through this venue. Extreme care should be used not to violate these laws as it is equally costly to defend antitrust actions. Moreover, if found guilty, violators could be required to pay a penalty equal to three times the actual damages.

Chapter 10 • Antitrust Considerations

CHAPTER 11

# Anti-Kickback and Self-Referral Laws

Many physicians and administrators refer generically to laws regulating physician referrals to facilities in which they have ownership interest as Stark laws. In reality, there are two critical laws—the Stark law and the anti-kickback statute. Many states have similar laws. Both laws are directed at the concern that inappropriate financial incentives will influence medical decision making. This similarity notwithstanding, the statutes are different in scope and structural approach. In the ASC context, it is the anti-kickback statute and not the Stark law that has the most significant impact. Specifically, and as noted below, ASCs that provide only ambulatory surgery services are in general not covered by the Stark law. In contrast, any ASC providing Medicare or Medicaid services is covered by the anti-kickback statute. Also worth noting, the anti-kickback statute is a criminal statute whereas the Stark law is a civil law. This means that violations of the anti-kickback statute can lead to imprisonment, as well as fines and loss of licensure.

## ANTI-KICKBACK STATUTE

Section 1128(b) of the Social Security Act, known as the anti-kickback statute, provides criminal penalties for individuals or entities that knowingly and willfully offer, pay, solicit or receive remuneration to induce business reimbursable under federal or state health care programs. The types of remuneration covered by the anti-kickback statute include commissions, kickbacks, bribes and rebates, whether made directly or indirectly, overtly or covertly, in cash or in kind. Violation of the anti-kickback statute is a felony and punishable by fines of up to $25,000 and imprisonment for up to five years. Violations of the anti-kickback statute may also result in the

**Protecting Your ASC: A Legal Handbook**　　　　　　　　**77**

imposition of a civil money penalty and/or exclusion from the Medicare and Medicaid programs.

Many physicians and administrators point to the fact that there have been very few prosecutions of ASCs under the anti-kickback statute as a reason not to be concerned with this statute. Moreover, the OIG has recognized the benefits that ASCs produce. For example, an OIG advisory opinion said:

> At the outset, we note that the Health Care Financing Administration [HCFA, now CMS] promotes ambulatory surgical centers as a cost-effective alternative to higher cost settings, such as hospital inpatient surgery facilities. Many patients prefer treatment in less intensive settings, such as ambulatory surgical centers. Thus, ambulatory surgical centers benefit both the Medicare program and its beneficiaries.[15]

The OIG continued expressing the view that

> [t]here are obvious and legitimate business and professional reasons for surgeons to want to own an ambulatory surgical center in which they will personally perform services on a routine basis. These reasons include personal and patient convenience, professional autonomy, accountability, and quality control. Moreover, any risk of overutilization or unnecessary surgery is already present by reason of the opportunity for a surgeon to generate his professional fee; the additional financial return from the ambulatory surgical centers investment is not likely to increase the risk of overutilization substantially.[16]

Before concluding, however, the OIG noted,

> Notwithstanding, this Office is concerned about the potential for investments in ambulatory surgical centers to serve as vehicles to reward referring physicians indirectly.[17]

Because of the severe consequences for violation of this law, the lack of prosecutions to date should not be seen as removing concerns for ASCs.

Many actions that would not immediately come to mind might be considered payments for referrals. For example:

- A partner or the ASC entity finances a physician's investment in an ASC.
- Parties disproportionately guarantee ASC debt or finance ASC operations, particularly if the parties receive nothing for their actions.
- An ASC provides for distributions or payments based on physician production or referrals.
- A management company is paid for bringing cases to an ASC.
- Patient copayments are waived to encourage use of the ASC.
- A physician is allowed to invest in the ASC to reward him or her for referrals to other physicians or the ASC.
- An ASC requires non-surgeons to refer patients to the ASC.
- A hospital invites doctors to invest in and refer to the ASC in

exchange for referrals to the hospital.

- Lease or other payments are made based on referrals.
- Employees are allowed to own shares in exchange for helping to bring patients to the ASC.
- Preferred returns are paid to physicians.
- The number of shares physicians can own is based on referrals.
- Physicians are given benefits such as free space at the ASC.

## SAFE HARBORS AND ADVISORY OPINIONS

Because of the difficulty of determining exactly what conduct violates the anti-kickback statute, Congress directed the OIG to issue *advisory opinions* and what are called *safe harbors*. Under the advisory opinion process, those involved in an arrangement or considering involvement in an arrangement can request an opinion from the OIG to determine whether or not the arrangement would violate the anti-kickback statute. Those requesting opinions must pay the costs. For information on how to request an advisory opinion, see FASA's Background Paper titled "The Anti-Kickback Statute." Such opinions are binding only on that specific arrangement and do not address state law issues. However, such opinions do offer insight into the government's view of situations and thus can be used in analyzing potential arrangements. Safe harbors are a specific set of criteria issued by the OIG to define arrangements that are not found to violate the antitrust laws. Full compliance with a safe harbor protects one from prosecution under the anti-kickback statute. However, failure to comply with a safe harbor does not mean that the arrangement violates the statute. If an owner is confident that the arrangement in question does not violate the statute, compliance with a safe harbor is not necessary. As of April 2001, there are 19 safe harbors, including a specific safe harbor for ASCs. In the commentary accompanying the final regulations establishing the ASC safe harbor, the OIG stated the rationale for the ASC safe harbor saying,

> Where the ASC is functionally an extension of the physician's office, so that the physician personally performs services at the ASC on his or her own patients as a substantial part of his or her medical practice, we believe that the ASC serves a *bona fide* business purpose and that the risk of improper payments for referrals is relatively low.[18]

The ASC safe harbor provides a starting point for analysis for ASCs wishing to have the assurance that they won't be charged with violating the anti-kickback statute. Many lawyers view it as good practice to comply with the safe harbor to the greatest extent practicable because, as a general

**Protecting Your ASC: A Legal Handbook**

rule, such compliance makes it less likely that a party will be prosecuted for violating the statute. However, absent full compliance, an ASC cannot be certain that its conduct or its operations will not be investigated, prosecuted or found to be illegal.

To qualify under the ASC safe harbor, the following conditions must be met:

- The ASC must be Medicare-certified.
- Loans from the entity or other investors for the purpose of investing are prohibited.
- Investment interest must be offered on terms not related to the volume or value of referrals.
- All ancillary services must be directly and integrally related to primary procedures performed at the ASC, and none may be separately billed to Medicare or other federal health care programs.
- Neither the ASC nor physicians practicing at the ASC can discriminate against federal health care program beneficiaries.
- Patients that are referred to an ASC by an investor physician must be fully informed of the investor's investment interest.

The four categories of ASCs that can be protected by the ASC safe harbor are

- surgeon-owned ASCs
- single-specialty ASCs
- multi-specialty ASCs
- hospital/physician ASCs

Compliance with the safe harbor requires an ASC to meet all requirements of the applicable category in addition to those described above.

To qualify under the surgeon-owned ASC category,[19] all the investors must be

- general surgeons or surgeons engaged in the same surgical specialty, all of whom are in a position to refer patients directly to the ASC and perform procedures on such referred patients;
- group practices that are composed of such surgeons and that meet all the requirements of the group practice safe harbor; or
- investors who
  1. do not provide items or services to the ASC or its investors;
  2. are not employed by the ASC or any investor; and
  3. are not in a position to refer patients directly or indirectly to, or generate business for, the ASC or any of its investors.

A surgeon is considered to be in a position to refer patients directly and perform procedures if he or she derives at least one-third of his or her medical practice income from all sources for the previous fiscal year or previous 12-month period from his or her own performance of procedures that require an ASC or hospital surgical setting in accordance with Medicare reimbursement rules (the one-third practice income test).

To qualify under the single-specialty ASC category,[20] all the investors must be

- physicians engaged in the same medical practice specialty who are in a position to refer patients directly to the ASC and perform procedures on such referred patients (such as gastroenterologists);
- group practices that are composed of such physicians and that meet all the requirements of the group practice safe harbor; or
- investors who
  1. do not provide items or services to the ASC or its investors;
  2. are not employed by the ASC or any investor; and
  3. are not in a position to refer patients directly or indirectly to, or generate business for, the ASC or any of its investors. As with surgeon-owned ASCs, physician investors must meet the one-third practice income test.

To qualify under the multi-specialty ASC category,[21] all the investors need to be

- physicians (surgeons or non-surgeons) who are in a position to refer patients directly to the ASC and perform procedures on such referred patients;
- group practices that are composed of such physicians and that meet all the requirements of the group practice safe harbor; or
- investors who
  1. do not provide items or services to the ASC or its investors;
  2. are not employed by the ASC or any investor; and
  3. are not in a position to refer patients directly or indirectly to, or generate business for, the ASC or any of its investors.

In this category, physician investors must meet the one-third practice income test described above as well as a second standard related to practice location. Specifically, the rule requires that at least one-third of the physician's procedures that require an ASC or hospital surgical setting (in accordance with Medicare reimbursement rules) be performed at the ASC in which he or she is investing. This one-third practice income/one-third

**Protecting Your ASC: A Legal Handbook** 81

practice location test is intended to ensure that an investment in an ASC truly qualifies as an extension of a physician's office.

To qualify for the hospital/physician ASC category,[22] at least one investor must be a hospital and the other investors must be

- physicians or group practices that otherwise qualify under the ASC safe harbor, or
- non-referral source investors, or
- non-employees.

The hospital must not be in a position to refer patients directly or indirectly to the ASC or any physician investor. The ASC space must be dedicated exclusively to the ASC and not used by the hospital for the treatment of the hospital's inpatients or outpatients. The ASC may lease space that is located in or owned by a hospital investor, if the space lease qualifies for protection under the space rental safe harbor. Equipment and personal services provided by the hospital must similarly meet safe harbor requirements.

## GUIDANCE IN INTERPRETING SAFE HARBORS

To ensure compliance with these requirements, ASCs have a number of choices. Physicians can be required to certify annually to the ASC that the physicians are in compliance with the safe harbors, including the one-third practice income and one-third practice location tests. Alternatively, the ASC can request practice data from physicians either annually or as a suspicion arises to help assess compliance with these requirements. In this situation, it is possible to include a provision having an independent third-party review the data and report to the ASC on compliance. Third, the board or ASC can do nothing to check compliance until a concern arises.

The OIG has taken the position that parties such as hospitals and management companies can refer patients. For purposes of the ASC safe harbor, this places both hospital-physician ventures and management company–physician ventures in a difficult position in trying to comply completely with the ASC safe harbor. The OIG said:

[W]e believe that hospitals, skilled nursing facilities, home health agencies, managed care companies, physician practice management companies, and similar entities may be referral sources in some circumstances. By way of example only, a hospital may be in a position to influence referrals when it employs physicians who make referrals, when it owns surgical practices, or when it is affiliated with a "friendly" or "captive" professional corporation owned or controlled by its employees. We further believe that some employees, such as certain marketing and administrative staff, may be referral sources.[23]

The requirement for disclosure of the surgeon's financial interest has raised numerous questions and concerns. The OIG has long encouraged the disclosure of financial interests by physicians to patients. While many physicians at first object to this practice, once they begin to use a patient disclosure process, they often find that it does not degrade their relationships with their patients whatsoever. It becomes a routine part of the consent process. Unfortunately, for ASCs, no guidance has been provided as to what *fully inform* means, or when or how the information should be exchanged. Many believe that this requirement can be met by the surgeon providing a form disclosing to the patient that the surgeon has an investment interest in the ASC and may receive profits from procedures performed in the ASC. It is the ASC that might be found to violate the law, so the ASC should require disclosure by all surgeons with financial interests.

## COMPENSATION ISSUES

ASCs have a wide range of compensation relationships with parties that could affect the ASC's success. For example, ASCs may hire referring physicians as medical directors, pay anesthesiologists who perform cases at the ASC and who also bring pain cases to the ASC, lease space or equipment from referring physicians, and pay management firms for their services. Many ASCs wrongly believe that the latitude the OIG has provided the ASCs with respect to physician ownership gives ASCs license to enter into very creative financial and compensation relationships with referring physicians. This is untrue and very risky. In fact, the OIG specifically noted the potential abuses of space rentals. In the commentary to the final regulation, the OIG stated:

> Several commenters . . . stated that sham office leases in which the space is not actually used are among the most common and abusive kickback schemes. Examples of such abusive schemes cited by commenters included physicians who entered into office rental contracts with other referring physicians, solely in order to obtain the referrals, and diagnostic services companies and clinical laboratories that lease space from physicians which the laboratories in reality do not use, as kickbacks for the physicians' patient referrals.[24]

The OIG elaborated on this issue, saying:

> We have become aware of office rental arrangements in which the "space" rented may not be large enough or otherwise suitable to perform any services for which rent could legitimately be paid. For example, a physician may rent office space to a clinical laboratory, allegedly in order to provide space to furnish laboratory services, when the space (often a closet or anteroom not useable for such purposes) is not actually occupied by laboratory personnel at any time. If the physician refers most or all laboratory work to this lessee, the "rent" is simply remuneration for referring laboratory work.[25]

**Protecting Your ASC: A Legal Handbook**

However, the OIG has also issued safe harbors for certain lease and management and services relationships. The equipment safe harbor rental and the space rental safe harbor includes criteria aimed at ensuring that the relationship is not intended to induce referrals. Specifically,

1. the term of the lease must be at least one year;
2. the aggregate rental charge and amounts to be paid under the lease must be set in advance;
3. the payment amount under the lease must be consistent with fair market value in an arm's-length transaction;
4. the amount of the rental charge must not take into account the volume or value of any referrals or business that may be generated between the partnership.

The OIG's commentary accompanying the safe harbor regulation explains the fair market value of criterion number 3 a little further, saying:

> The safe harbor provision for space rental does not contemplate a single figure for fair market value. Rather, it contemplates a rental fee falling within a reasonable commercial range, but not taking into account any value attached by either party based upon the property's proximity or convenience to referral sources. To the extent there is a nexus between the location of property and the opportunity to engage in business reimbursable under Medicare or Medicaid, rental charges that take location into account may impermissibly generate referrals or other health care business. For example, we believe that a fair inference may be drawn that impermissible payments are being made when a group of doctors owns a medical arts building and rents space in that building to a diagnostic laboratory, and the rent is substantially above the laboratory's cost of renting the same sized space at a nearby location.[26]

The commentary also makes clear that the costs of making the space suitable for the furnishing of medical services (such as extra plumbing or electrical costs) should be considered in determining fair market value.

Based upon the last criterion, these safe harbors do not permit per use payments or payments that vary based on the volume or value of business done by the ASC.

The requirements to comply with the safe harbor for personal services and for management contracts are very similar to those requirements set forth for renting space or renting equipment. Specifically, for personal service arrangements and for management agreements, the principal standards require

1. aggregate compensation must be set in advance;
2. the compensation must be consistent with fair market value in an arm's-length transaction; and
3. the payment amount cannot take into account the volume or value of any referrals generated between the parties.

This last criterion is problematic. The standard throughout the ASC industry has been to pay for management services on a percentage basis. Generally, ASCs pay management companies anywhere between four percent and nine percent for the provision of administrative and management services. Payment made on a percentage basis generally does not comply with the safe harbor. Moreover, in an advisory opinion and in certain commentary on the safe harbors, the OIG has raised concerns with regard to payment relationships based on a percentage amount. Hence, when a party pays for management services on a percentage basis, one must be extremely careful to ensure that the services paid for do not include the bringing of patients or the referral of patients, directly or indirectly, to the ASC or to the surgeons.

In Advisory Opinion 98-4 issued April 15, 1998, the OIG expressed concern with such arrangements, stating:

> The Proposed Arrangement may include financial incentives to increase patient referrals. The compensation that Company B receives for its management services is a percentage of Company A's net revenue, including revenue from business derived from managed care contracts arranged by Company B. Such activities may potentially implicate the Anti-Kickback Statute, because the compensation Company B will receive will be in part for marketing services. Where such compensation is based on a percentage, there is at least a potential technical violation of the Anti-Kickback Statute. In addition, Company B will be establishing networks of specialist physicians to whom Company A may be required to refer in some circumstances.

Evidence of CMS's disfavor toward percentage compensation arrangements can also be found within the Medicare billing regulations. The regulations specifically prohibit Medicare payment to agents that furnish billing and collection services to providers where the agent's compensation is related in any way to the dollar amounts billed or collected.[27] This prohibition suggests that CMS is concerned that payments based on how much business the provider generates encourages an agent acting on a physician's behalf to work harder to increase the business performed by the physician. This sort of behavior might be interpreted as a manifestation of the intent to refer business and, therefore, violates the fraud and abuse statute.

Because compensation methods that base payment upon the volume of business generated have potential fraud and abuse implications, ASCs should consider entering into payment arrangements that are fixed, such as flat-fee arrangements, particularly when contracting to receive services from potential referral sources, or when contracting with third parties to perform administrative or management functions for them.

**Protecting Your ASC: A Legal Handbook**

Another area of potential fraud and abuse concern arises in the context of an arrangement between a hospital and an ASC through which the ASC sends patients for tests to be performed in the hospital's laboratory for surgical procedures that are performed at the ASC. CMS has suggested that ASCs may, in fact, make arrangements with an independent laboratory or other laboratory, such as a hospital laboratory, to perform diagnostic tests prior to surgery.[28] However, an arrangement between an ASC and a hospital through which the ASC agrees to send patients to the hospital's laboratory could be perceived as the ASC offering the hospital an inducement to refer cases to the ASC. ASCs should not interpret this to mean that they cannot send patients to hospital laboratories for diagnostic testing prior to surgery, as noted above, CMS has stated that this may be permitted. ASCs should, however, ensure that the preoperative testing is actually medically necessary and not a condition to receiving the referral for the surgical case from the physician or hospital.

## WAIVER OF COPAYMENTS AND DEDUCTIBLES

In many situations, ASCs want to waive patients' copayments or deductibles. The concept may be that by waiving copayments or deductibles, an ASC can eliminate a disincentive to the patient choosing the ASC for his or her surgery. As a general rule, it is illegal to offer a Medicare beneficiary patient a waiver of a copayment or deductible to induce the patient to use the ASC for his or her surgical care. However, a waiver is permissible when it is intended to help indigent patients afford surgery. Those setting up a program should review OIG guidance in Advisory Opinions 99-6 and 99-7. For private pay patients, you may be able to waive copayments or deductibles. However, many state laws prohibit or regulate such waivers. Moreover, insurance contracts may prohibit waivers.

## POINTERS TO AVOID ANTI-KICKBACK VIOLATIONS

Absent existing ownership, or an unusual situation, primary care physicians and other indirect referral sources should generally not be asked to invest in ASCs. The OIG, in commentary accompanying the ASC safe harbor regulations, explained the problem with primary care investors:

> Two examples illustrate the potential problem. First, primary care physicians could be offered an investment interest in an ASC for a nominal capital contribution as an incentive to refer patients to surgeon owners of the ASC. The primary care physicians would not perform any services at the ASC, but would profit from any referrals they

make. Second, physicians in specialties that typically refer to one another could jointly invest in an ASC so that they are positioned to earn a profit from such referrals or so that one physician specialty provides the ASC services and the other provides the referrals. In such cases, medical decision-making may be corrupted by financial incentives offered to potential referral sources who stand to profit from services provided by another physician.[29]

Other recommendations include the following:

- The existing primary care ownership should be demonstrated to be unrelated to any purpose to attract or reward referrals. No referrals to surgeons by primary care physicians should be conditioned on use of the ASC.

- Hospitals should state in writing that they will not direct or steer business to the ASC.

- Hospital partners or managers should not require the ASC or physicians to refer to the hospital.

- Physicians may be required to attest that they qualify as *surgeons*. In the multi-specialty setting, physicians may have to attest that they will use the ASC as an extension of their practice. Here, the ASC may need to audit surgeon practice if questions arise to prove that a person is a surgeon and meeting the requirements.

- Disclosure of investment interests should be made to patients.

- Distribution of income should be made based on ownership and not based on referrals or production.

- Management companies should be permitted to invest only if they will not be significantly involved in marketing activities.

- Investors should generally be offered equal investment opportunities.

- Other investors or the entity should not help an investor finance his or her investment in the ASC.

- All leases and all directorship relationships should be fixed at fair market value and should meet a real need of the ASC.

- Valuations may be obtained to show that transactions and compensation relationships are at fair market value.

- All investors buying investments at the same time should generally pay the same per-share amount for investments.

- ASCs should adopt and follow a health care regulatory compliance plan.

- Any percentage-based agreements should be clearly documented as not related to referrals or marketing.

**Protecting Your ASC: A Legal Handbook**

- Ownership by physicians, absent special circumstances, should be limited to surgeons and doctors who perform surgical procedures and who practice at the ASC.

## STARK LAW

The Stark law, unlike the anti-kickback statute, has limited applicability to most ASCs. The Stark law is a civil statute that generally (1) prohibits physicians from making referrals for designated health services (described below) to entities in which those physicians have ownership or other financial interests and (2) prohibits entities from presenting or causing to be presented claims or bills to any individual, third-party payer or other entity for designated health services furnished pursuant to a prohibited referral. Services covered by the Stark law are only those specifically defined as *designated health services* in the law. These are clinical laboratory services; physical therapy services; occupational therapy services; radiology services, including magnetic resonance imaging, computerized axial tomography scans and ultrasound services; radiation therapy services and supplies; durable medical equipment and supplies; parenteral and enteral nutrients, equipment and supplies; prosthetics, orthodontics and prosthetic devices and supplies; home health services; outpatient prescription drugs; and inpatient and outpatient hospital services. Surgical services in an ASC are not covered. While ASCs may provide a small portion of covered services under their composite rate, those services that are not separately billed to the Medicare or Medicaid programs are not covered by the Stark law.

The Stark law does have specific impact on situations in which hospitals operate hospital outpatient departments or hospital-owned ASCs and attempt to provide special compensation to physicians.

Under the Stark law, physicians may not refer patients for designated health services to entities from which the physicians receive financial benefits, except as allowed in enumerated exceptions. A transaction must fall entirely within an exception to be lawful under the Stark law.

Notwithstanding the potential inclusion of certain services, the Stark law has been clarified to exclude "services furnished in an ASC if payment for those services is included in the ASC payment rate." The law remains applicable to services that appear on the list of those provided in an ASC and are not included in the global fee hospital surgical programs and other reimbursable services.

# CONCLUSION

ASCs must pay close attention to complying with anti-kickback regulations. There are severe consequences for violating these provisions. ASCs and ASC investors must also comply with state laws regulating physician referrals to facilities in which they have financial interests. In general, ASCs are not covered by the Stark law.

90             Chapter 11 • Anti-Kickback and Self-Referral Laws

# CHAPTER 12

# False Claims Act

The False Claims Act (FCA) has become an increasingly important law for the health care community. The FCA provides that anyone who knowingly presents a false claim to the government for payment may be liable for a minimum civil penalty of $5,000 and a maximum penalty of $10,000 per claim plus three times the actual damages or treble damages. The FCA can be violated by making an error on the CMS Form 855, coding certain procedures at a higher level than appropriate, undercoding certain procedures, improperly billing and submitting any Medicare or other government claim that contains an error.

*Knowing* and *knowingly* are defined under the FCA to mean that a person either has (1) actual knowledge of the falsity of the claim, (2) acts in deliberate ignorance of the truth or falsity of the claim or (3) acts in reckless disregard of the truth or falsity of the claim. The FCA requires no proof of specific intent to defraud. The FCA defines a *claim* as any request or demand for money or property made to a contractor, grantee or other recipient if the government provides any portion of such money or property or if the government reimburses such contractor, grantee or other recipient for any portion of money or property requested or demanded.

Under the FCA, individuals with knowledge of the false claim, such as employees, former employees or patients, may file an action on behalf of the government, a so-called *qui tam* lawsuit. Such individuals receive a share of the proceeds if the lawsuit is successful. Because of this incentive, it is increasingly common for employees or former employees to bring such suits. One ASC was found to violate this act due to a claim made by a potential employee following a job interview during which she observed activities that resulted in false claims.

The government, as well as *qui tam* plaintiffs, use a variety of theories to allege that a provider has violated the FCA. Specifically, FCA liability may

**Protecting Your ASC: A Legal Handbook**                                                **91**

be triggered when (1) providers submit claims for medically unnecessary services, (2) providers use improper coding or billing practices, (3) a provider submits a claim for services not provided or covered under a federal program, (4) a provider excluded from a federal program submits claims, (5) a provider violates a statute or regulation, (6) a provider falsely certifies it has complied with certain statutes or regulations or (7) a provider submits claims for services that do not meet quality-of-care standards.

## MEDICALLY UNNECESSARY SERVICES

As a general condition of participation in the Medicare program, ASCs are required to certify that the services they perform are medically necessary.[30] Similarly, by executing CMS Form 1500, a physician or supplier certifies that the services for which reimbursement is sought were medically necessary. Accordingly, FCA liability may be triggered when providers submit Medicare claims to the government for reimbursement in connection with services that are not medically necessary. Here, the main potential for liability exists in situations where an ASC is reckless with regard to the medical necessity determination actions of its physicians or encourages in some way performance of surgery or a second procedure regardless of medical necessity. ASCs should have policies that prohibit the performance of medically unnecessary procedures on Medicare patients and may want to have physicians attest to each procedure's medical necessity when submitting billing information.

## IMPROPER CODING AND BILLING PRACTICES

Improper coding and billing practices that may generate FCA liability include upcoding, downcoding, unbundling and presumptive coding. One case of note is *United States v. Krizek*.[31] Here, the defendant's billing was performed by his wife and another assistant. The two clerks would prepare each claim using the same code without consulting the physician to confirm that the code was appropriate. Indeed, the court found that the clerks prepared the claims with little or no factual basis and often had no justification for using the code in question.

In the ASC setting, rules that should be followed at a minimum include the following:

- Coding must match the chart, not the presumption of the services performed.
- Coders should have reasonable time to complete their efforts and not have unreasonable quotas.

- Surgeons should be accessible for questions.
- Third-party education and manuals should be available.
- Education should be regular.

## CLAIMS FOR SERVICES NOT COVERED UNDER A FEDERAL PROGRAM

Other types of false claims under the FCA include billing the government for services not covered by a federal program. In *United States v. Lorenzo*,[32] the defendant-dentists had been giving patients routine dental exams that included oral cancer screenings. Such routine exams, however, were not reimbursable under Medicare. To receive Medicare reimbursement, therefore, the dentists would classify the screenings as *limited consultations*, which were covered under Medicare. However, the court found that oral cancer screenings were properly considered part of the routine dental exam and, therefore, not Medicare reimbursable. Accordingly, the court found that the dentists violated the FCA.

## BILLING FOR SERVICES OF EXCLUDED PROVIDER

Liability will also be triggered under the FCA when a provider who has been excluded from participation in a federal program submits a claim for reimbursement. Here, ASCs should be able to avoid exposure through a regular credentialing process.

## STATUTORY OR REGULATORY VIOLATION

Some courts have found that violation of state licensure, CON, Medicare certification or the Stark or anti-kickback laws may trigger FCA liability. In *United States ex rel. Pogue v. American Healthcorp, Inc.*,[33] the *qui tam* relator alleged that the government would not have paid the defendant's Medicare claims if the government had known the claims were premised on the defendants' Stark and anti-kickback violations and thus were false claims. The court noted that, based on such allegations, it appeared as if the defendants concealed their prohibited activities so that the government would pay the claims. The court held that liability attaches under the FCA if defendants engage in fraudulent activity to induce payment from the government. Accordingly, the court found that the relator had sufficiently stated a claim for relief under the FCA. Notably, the court also stated that the FCA is not implicated if the fraudulent activity in question was not performed to induce government payment.

Similarly, it has been argued that false or implied certification of compliance with Medicare or other laws and regulations may create FCA liability. Under this theory, claims are deemed fraudulent if a provider certifies compliance with Medicare laws or regulations, or other laws and regulations, in connection with submitting claims to the government when in fact the provider is not in compliance.

It is important to note that FCA liability under a false or implied certification theory is not established solely on the basis of regulatory or statutory transgressions. Rather, it is the false certification of compliance with such laws and regulations that creates FCA liability. In US *Joslin v. Community Home Health of Maryland*,[34] the *qui tam* relator claimed that the defendant violated the FCA because it had not complied with state licensure requirements as mandated under the Medicare conditions of participation for home health care providers. Here, the court found that the form defendants used to submit their Medicare claims did not contain a certification that defendants were in compliance with state laws. The court reasoned that non-compliance with a statute or regulation alone does not constitute, without any false certifications, a false statement under the FCA. Accordingly, defendants were not liable for violating the FCA. Alternatively, the relator argued that the mere submission of Medicare claims qualifies as an implied certification that defendants have complied with any applicable statutes and regulations. The court disagreed, however, holding that following such a rule ignores the principle that the FCA is not designed to punish every type of fraud committed against the government. Moreover, the court noted that the theory of "implied certification" ignores the FCA's intent requirement. In *Luckey v. Baxter Healthcare Corp.*,[35] the defendant manufactured plasma products. As a requirement for obtaining a license to make such products, the defendant certified that it was in compliance with certain federal regulations. The *qui tam* relator alleged the defendant violated the FCA because by submitting claims to the government for payment, it implicitly certified that it was complying with the applicable regulations. In this case, the court rejected the argument.

## SERVICES NOT MEETING THE STANDARD OF CARE

Finally, the government will pursue providers for a violation of the FCA for claims submitted for services that fail to meet an appropriate standard of quality care. In *United States ex rel. Aranda v. Community Psychiatric Centers of Oklahoma, Inc.*,[36] the government alleged the defendant violated the FCA because when the defendant submitted claims for reimbursement under the Medicaid program, it implicitly certified that it provided patients with an "appropriate quality of care and a safe and secure environment." The government argued that patients had suffered physical injury and sexual abuse because the defendant had failed to provide a safe environment for its patients. The defendant argued that the government did not adequately state a claim under the FCA because failure to follow an appropriate standard of care is not a billing requirement for reimbursement. The court noted, however, that Medicaid statutes and regulations do require providers to meet quality of care standards. If such standards are not met, a provider may be excluded from the program. Accordingly, the court found that the government's allegations were sufficient to establish an FCA claim.

## CONCLUSION

ASC employees must understand what part they play in satisfying the requirements of the False Claims Act. It is important to note that individuals—such as employees, former employees and patients—may allege that an ASC is in violation of the False Claims Act and receive a percentage of the proceeds if the ASC is found guilty and has to pay penalties. Accordingly, it is prudent to educate employees so that they understand the ASC is complying with the law. Moreover, it is wise to provide a service, such as a hotline, for employees to use to convey concerns and for the ASC managers to use to address complaints raised.

**Protecting Your ASC: A Legal Handbook**

# Appendix A

## State Certificate of Need (CON) Laws
August 2001

### CON laws applicable to at least some ASC Projects (28)

| | | |
|---|---|---|
| Alabama | Maine | North Carolina |
| Alaska | Maryland | Rhode Island |
| Connecticut | Massachusetts | South Carolina |
| Delaware | Michigan | Tennessee |
| District of Columbia | Mississippi | Vermont |
| Georgia | Missouri[1] | Virginia |
| Hawaii | Montana | Washington |
| Illinois | Nevada[2] | West Virginia |
| Iowa | New Hampshire | |
| Kentucky | New York | |

### CON laws not applicable to ASCs (9)

| | | |
|---|---|---|
| Arkansas | Nebraska | Oklahoma |
| Florida | New Jersey | Oregon |
| Louisiana | Ohio | Wisconsin |

### No CON Law (14)

| | | |
|---|---|---|
| Arizona | Kansas | South Dakota |
| California | Minnesota | Texas |
| Colorado | New Mexico | Utah |
| Idaho | North Dakota | Wyoming |
| Indiana | Pennsylvania | |

---

[1] Only if ASC includes major medical equipment of more than $1 million.

[2] Las Vegas, Reno and all counties with a population of more than 100,000 are exempt.

# Appendix B

## Medicare ASC Regulations
42 CFR Part 416

### Sec. 416.1 Basis and scope.

(a) *Statutory basis.* (1) Section 1832(a)(2)(F)(i) of the Act provides for Medicare Part B coverage of facility services furnished in connection with surgical procedures specified by the Secretary under section 1833(i)(1) of the Act.

(2) Section 1833(i)(1)(A) of the Act requires the Secretary to specify the surgical procedures that can be performed safely on an ambulatory basis in an ambulatory surgical center, or a hospital outpatient department.

(3) Section[s] 1833(i) (2)(A) and (3) specify the amounts to be paid for facility services furnished in connection with the specified surgical procedures when they are performed, respectively, in an ASC, or in a hospital outpatient department.

(b) *Scope.* This part sets forth—

(1) The conditions that an ASC must meet in order to participate in the Medicare program;

(2) The scope of covered services; and

(3) The conditions for Medicare payment for facility services.

[56 FR 8843, Mar. 1, 1991; 56 FR 23022, May 20, 1991]

### Sec. 416.2 Definitions.

As used in this part:

*Ambulatory surgical center* or *ASC* means any distinct entity that operates exclusively for the purpose of providing surgical services to patients not requiring hospitalization, has an agreement with HCFA to participate in Medicare as an ASC, and meets the conditions set forth in subparts B and C of this part. *ASC services* means facility services that are furnished in an ASC.

*Covered surgical procedures* means those surgical and other medical procedures that meet the criteria specified in Sec. 416.65 and are published by HCFA in the FEDERAL REGISTER.

Protecting Your ASC: A Legal Handbook     97

*Facility services* means services that are furnished in connection with covered surgical procedures performed in an ASC, or in a hospital on an outpatient basis.

[56 FR 8843, Mar. 1, 1991; 56 FR 23022, May 20, 1991]

## Sec. 416.25 Basic requirements.

Participation as an ASC is limited to facilities that—
(a) Meet the definition in Sec. 416.2; and
(b) Have in effect an agreement obtained in accordance with this subpart.

[56 FR 8843, Mar. 1, 1991]

## Sec. 416.26 Qualifying for an agreement.

(a) *Deemed compliance.* HCFA may deem an ASC to be in compliance with any or all of the conditions set forth in subpart C of this part if—

(1) The ASC is accredited by a national accrediting body, or licensed by a State agency, that HCFA determines provides reasonable assurance that the conditions are met;

(2) In the case of deemed status through accreditation by a national accrediting body, where State law requires licensure, the ASC complies with State licensure requirements; and

(3) The ASC authorizes the release to HCFA, of the findings of the accreditation survey.

(b) *Survey of ASCs.* (1) Unless HCFA deems the ASC to be in compliance with the conditions set forth in subpart C of this part, the State survey agency must survey the facility to ascertain compliance with those conditions, and report its findings to HCFA.

(2) HCFA surveys deemed ASCs on a sample basis as part of HCFA's validation process.

(c) *Acceptance of the ASC as qualified to furnish ambulatory surgical services.* If HCFA determines, after reviewing the survey agency recommendation and other evidence relating to the qualification of the ASC, that the facility meets the requirements of this part, it sends to the ASC—

(1) Written notice of the determination; and

(2) Two copies of the ASC agreement.

(d) *Filing of agreement by the ASC.* If the ASC wishes to participate in the program, it must—

(1) Have both copies of the ASC agreement signed by its authorized representative; and

(2) File them with HCFA.

(e) *Acceptance by HCFA.* If HCFA accepts the agreement filed by the ASC, returns to the ASC one copy of the agreement, with a notice of acceptance specifying the effective date.

(f) *Appeal rights.* If HCFA refuses to enter into an agreement or if HCFA terminates an agreement, the ASC is entitled to a hearing in accordance with part 498 of this chapter.

[56 FR 8843, Mar. 1, 1991]

## Sec. 416.30 Terms of agreement with HCFA.

As part of the agreement under Sec. 416.26 the ASC must agree to the following:

(a) *Compliance with coverage conditions.* The ASC agrees to meet the conditions for coverage specified in subpart C of this part and to report promptly to HCFA any failure to do so.

(b) *Limitation on charges to beneficiaries.*[1] The ASC agrees to charge the beneficiary or any other person only the applicable deductible and coinsurance amounts for facility services for which the beneficiary

(1) Is entitled to have payment made on his or her behalf under this part; or

(2) Would have been so entitled if the ASC had filed a request for payment in accordance with Sec. 410.165 of this chapter.

(c) *Refunds to beneficiaries.* (1) The ASC agrees to refund as promptly as possible any money incorrectly collected from beneficiaries or from someone on their behalf.

(2) As used in this section, *money incorrectly collected* means sums collected in excess of those specified in paragraph (b) of this section. It includes amounts collected for a period of time when the beneficiary was believed not to be entitled to Medicare benefits if—

(i) The beneficiary is later determined to have been entitled to Medicare benefits; and

(ii) The beneficiary's entitlement period falls within the time the ASC's agreement with HCFA is in effect.

---

[1]For facility services furnished before July 1987, the ASC had to agree to make no charge to the beneficiary, since those services were not subject to the part B deductible and coinsurance provisions.

**Protecting Your ASC: A Legal Handbook**

(d) *Furnishing information.* The ASC agrees to furnish to HCFA, if requested, information necessary to establish payment rates specified in Secs. 416.120-416.130 in the form and manner that HCFA requires.

(e) *Acceptance of assignment.* The ASC agrees to accept assignment for all facility services furnished in connection with covered surgical procedures. For purposes of this section, assignment means an assignment under Sec. 424.55 of this chapter of the right to receive payment under Medicare Part B and payment under Sec. 424.64 of this chapter (when an individual dies before assigning the claim).

(f) *ASCs operated by a hopsital* [*sic*]. In an ASC operated by a hospital—

(1) The agreement is made effective on the first day of the next Medicare cost reporting period of the hospital that operates the ASC; and

(2) The ASC participates and is paid only as an ASC, without the option of converting to or being paid as a hospital outpatient department, unless HCFA determines there is good cause to do otherwise.

(3) Costs for the ASC are treated as a non-reimbursable cost center on the hopsital's [*sic*] cost report.

(g) *Additional provisions.* The agreement may contain any additional provisions that HCFA finds necessary or desirable for the efficient and effective administration of the Medicare program.

[47 FR 34094, Aug. 5, 1982, as amended at 51 FR 41351, Nov. 14, 1986; 56 FR 8844, Mar. 1, 1991]

## Sec. 416.35 Termination of agreement.

(a) *Termination by the ASC*—(1) *Notice to HCFA.* An ASC that wishes to terminate its agreement must send HCFA written notice of its intent.

(2) *Date of termination.* The notice may state the intended date of termination which must be the first day of a calendar month.

(i) If the notice does not specify a date, or the date is not acceptable to HCFA, HCFA may set a date that will not be more than 6 months from the date on the ASC's notice of intent.

(ii) HCFA may accept a termination date that is less than 6

months after the date on the ASC's notice if it determines that to do so would not unduly disrupt services to the community or otherwise interfere with the effective and efficient administration of the Medicare program.

(3) *Voluntary termination.* If an ASC ceases to furnish services to the community, that shall be deemed to be a voluntary termination of the agreement by the ASC, effective on the last day of business with Medicare beneficiaries.

(b) *Termination by HCFA*—(1) *Cause for termination.* HCFA may terminate an agreement if it determines that the ASC—

(i) No longer meets the conditions for coverage as specified under Sec. 416.26; or

(ii) Is not in substantial compliance with the provisions of the agreement, the requirements of this subpart, and other applicable regulations of subchapter B of this chapter, or any applicable provisions of title XVIII of the Act.

(2) *Notice of termination.* HCFA sends notice of termination to the ASC at least 15 days before the effective date stated in the notice.

(3) *Appeal by the ASC.* An ASC may appeal the termination of its agreement in accordance with the provisions set forth in part 498 of this chapter.

(c) *Effect of termination.* Payment is not available for ASC services furnished on or after the effective date of termination.

(d) *Notice to the public.* Prompt notice of the date and effect of termination is given to the public, through publication in local newspapers by—

(1) The ASC, after HCFA has approved or set a termination date; or

(2) HCFA, when it has terminated the agreement.

(e) *Conditions for reinstatement after termination of agreement by HCFA.* When an agreement with an ASC is terminated by HCFA, the ASC may not file another agreement to participate in the Medicare program unless HCFA—

(1) Finds that the reason for the termination of the prior agreement has been removed; and

(2) Is assured that the reason for the termination will not recur.

[47 FR 34094, Aug. 5, 1982, as amended at 52 FR 22454, June 12, 1987; 56 FR 8844, Mar. 1, 1991; 61 FR 40347, Aug. 2, 1996]

---

**Protecting Your ASC: A Legal Handbook**

# Sec. 416.40 Condition for coverage—Compliance with State licensure law.

The ASC must comply with State licensure requirements.

# Sec. 416.41 Condition for coverage—Governing body and management.

The ASC must have a governing body, that assumes full legal responsibility for determining, implementing, and monitoring policies governing the ASC's total operation and for ensuring that these policies are administered so as to provide quality health care in a safe environment. When services are provided through a contract with an outside resource, the ASC must assure that these services are provided in a safe and effective manner. *Standard: Hospitalization.* The ASC must have an effective procedure for the immediate transfer to a hospital, of patients requiring emergency medical care beyond the capabilities of the ASC. This hospital must be a local, Medicare participating hospital or a local, nonparticipating hospital that meets the requirements for payment for emergency services under Sec. 482.2 of this chapter. The ASC must have a written transfer agreement with such a hospital, or all physicians performing surgery in the ASC must have admitting privileges at such a hospital.

[47 FR 34094, Aug. 5, 1982, as amended at 51 FR 22041, June 17, 1986]

# Sec. 416.42 Condition for coverage—Surgical services.

Surgical procedures must be performed in a safe manner by qualified physicians who have been granted clinical privileges by the governing body of the ASC in accordance with approved policies and procedures of the ASC.

(a) *Standard: Anesthetic risk and evaluation.* A physician must examine the patient immediately before surgery to evaluate the risk of anesthesia and of the procedure to be performed. Before discharge from the ASC, each patient must be evaluated by a physician for proper anesthesia recovery.

(b) *Standard: Administration of anesthesia.* Anesthetics must be administered by only —

(1) A qualified anesthesiologist; or

(2) A physician qualified to administer anesthesia, a certified

registered nurse anesthetist (CRNA) or an anesthesiologist's assistant as defined in §410.69(b) of this chapter, or a supervised trainee in an approved educational program. In those cases in which a non-physician administers the anesthesia, unless exempted in accordance with paragraph (d) of this section, the anesthetist must be under the supervision of the operating physician, and in the case of an anesthesiologist's assistant, under the supervision of an anesthesiologist.

(c) *Standard: Discharge.* All patients are discharged in the company of a responsible adult, except those exempted by the attending physician.

(d) *Standard: State exemption.* (1) An ASC may be exempted from the requirement for physician supervision of CRNAs as described in paragraph (b)(2) of this section, if the State in which the ASC is located submits a letter to CMS signed by the Governor, following consultation with the State's Boards of Medicine and Nursing, requesting exemption from physician supervision of CRNAs. The letter from the Governor must attest that he or she has consulted with State Boards of Medicine and Nursing about issues related to access to and the quality of anesthesia services in the State and has concluded that it is in the best interests of the State's citizens to opt-out of the current physician supervision requirement, and that the opt-out is consistent with State law.

(2) The request for exemption and recognition of State laws, and the withdrawal of the request may be submitted at any time, and are effective upon submission.

[57 FR 33899, July 31, 1992, as amended at 66 FR 56768, Nov. 13, 2001.]

# Sec. 416.43 Condition for coverage—Evaluation of quality.

The ASC, with the active participation of the medical staff, must conduct an ongoing, comprehensive self-assessment of the quality of care provided, including medical necessity of procedures performed and appropriateness of care, and use findings, when appropriate, in the revision of center policies and consideration of clinical privileges.

# Sec. 416.44 Condition for coverage—Environment.

The ASC must have a safe and sanitary environment, properly constructed, equipped, and maintained to protect the health and safety of patients.

(a) *Standard: Physical environment.* The ASC must provide a functional and sanitary environment for the provision of surgical services.

(1) Each operating room must be designed and equipped so that the types of surgery conducted can be performed in a manner that protects the lives and assures the physical safety of all individuals in the area.

(2) The ASC must have a separate recovery room and waiting area.

(3) The ASC must establish a program for identifying and preventing infections, maintaining a sanitary environment, and reporting the results to appropriate authorities.

(b) *Standard: Safety from fire.*

(1) Except as provided in paragraphs (b) (2) and (3) of this section, the ASC must meet the provisions of the 1985 edition of the Life Safety Code of the National Fire Protection Association (which is incorporated by reference)[1] that are applicable to ambulatory surgical centers.

(2) In consideration of a recommendation by the State survey agency, HCFA may waive, for periods deemed appropriate, specific provisions of the Life Safety Code which, if rigidly applied, would result in unreasonable hardship upon an ASC, but only if the waiver will not adversely affect the health and safety of the patients.

(3) Any ASC that, on May 9, 1988, complies with the requirements of the 1981 edition of the Life Safety Code, with or without waivers, will be considered to be in compliance with this standard, so long as the ASC continues to remain in compliance with that edition of the Life Safety Code.

(c) *Standard: Emergency equipment.* Emergency equipment available to the operating rooms must include at least the following:

(1) Emergency call system.

(2) Oxygen.

(3) Mechanical ventilatory assistance equipment including airways, manual breathing bag, and ventilator.

(4) Cardiac defibrillator.

(5) Cardiac monitoring equipment.

(6) Tracheostomy set.

(7) Laryngoscopes and endotracheal tubes.

(8) Suction equipment.

(9) Emergency medical equipment and supplies specified by the medical staff.

(d) *Standard: Emergency personnel.* Personnel trained in the use of emergency equipment and in cardiopulmonary resuscitation must be available whenever there is a patient in the ASC.

[47 FR 34094, Aug. 5, 1982, amended at 53 FR 11508, Apr. 7, 1988; 54 FR 4026, Jan. 27, 1989]

¹See footnote to Sec. 405.1134(a) of this chapter.

## Sec. 416.45 Condition for coverage—Medical staff.

The medical staff of the ASC must be accountable to the governing body.

(a) *Standard: Membership and clinical privileges.* Members of the medical staff must be legally and professionally qualified for the positions to which they are appointed and for the performance of privileges granted. The ASC grants privileges in accordance with recommendations from qualified medical personnel.

(b) *Standard: Reappraisals.* Medical staff privileges must be periodically reappraised by the ASC. The scope of procedures performed in the ASC must be periodically reviewed and amended as appropriate.

(c) *Standard: Other practitioners.* If the ASC assigns patient care responsibilities to practitioners other than physicians, it must have established policies and procedures, approved by the governing body, for overseeing and evaluating their clinical activities.

## Sec. 416.46 Condition for coverage—Nursing services.

The nursing services of the ASC must be directed and staffed to assure that the nursing needs of all patients are met.

(a) *Standard: Organization and staffing.* Patient care responsibilities must be delineated for all nursing service personnel. Nursing

Protecting Your ASC: A Legal Handbook

105

services must be provided in accordance with recognized standards of practice. There must be a registered nurse available for emergency treatment whenever there is a patient in the ASC.

(b) [Reserved]

## Sec. 416.47  Condition for coverage—Medical records.

The ASC must maintain complete, comprehensive, and accurate medical records to ensure adequate patient care.

(a) *Standard: Organization.* The ASC must develop and maintain a system for the proper collection, storage, and use of patient records.

(b) *Standard: Form and content of record.* The ASC must maintain a medical record for each patient. Every record must be accurate, legible, and promptly completed. Medical records must include at least the following:

(1) Patient identification.

(2) Significant medical history and results of physical examination.

(3) Pre-operative diagnostic studies (entered before surgery), if performed.

(4) Findings and techniques of the operation, including a pathologist's report on all tissues removed during surgery, except those exempted by the governing body.

(5) Any allergies and abnormal drug reactions.

(6) Entries related to anesthesia administration.

(7) Documentation of properly executed informed patient consent.

(8) Discharge diagnosis.

## Sec. 416.48  Condition for coverage—Pharmaceutical services.

The ASC must provide drugs and biologicals in a safe and effective manner, in accordance with accepted professional practice, and under the direction of an individual designated responsible for pharmaceutical services.

(a) *Standard: Administration of drugs.* Drugs must be prepared and administered according to established policies and acceptable standards of practice.

(1) Adverse reactions must be reported to the physician responsible for the patient and must be documented in the record.

(2) Blood and blood products must be administered by only physicians or registered nurses.

(3) Orders given orally for drugs and biologicals must be followed by a written order, signed by the prescribing physician.

(b) [Reserved]

## Sec. 416.49 Condition for coverage—Laboratory and radiologic services.

If the ASC performs laboratory services, it must meet the requirements of part 493 of this chapter. If the ASC does not provide its own laboratory services, it must have procedures for obtaining routine and emergency laboratory services from a certified laboratory in accordance with part 493 of this chapter. The referral laboratory must be certified in the appropriate specialties and subspecialties of service to perform the referred tests in accordance with the requirements of part 493 of this chapter. The ASC must have procedures for obtaining radiologic services from a Medicare approved facility to meet the needs of patients.

[57 FR 7135, Feb. 28, 1992]

## Sec. 416.60 General rules.

(a) The services payable under this part are facility services furnished to Medicare beneficiaries, by a participating facility, in connection with covered surgical procedures specified in Sec. 416.65.

(b) The surgical procedures, including all preoperative and post-operative services that are performed by a physician, are covered as physician services under part 410 of this chapter.

[56 FR 8844, Mar. 1, 1991]

## Sec. 416.61 Scope of facility services.

(a) *Included services.* Facility services include, but are not limited to—

(1) Nursing, technician, and related services;

(2) Use of the facilities where the surgical procedures are performed;

(3) Drugs, biologicals, surgical dressings, supplies, splints, casts, and appliances and equipment directly related to the provision of surgical procedures;

**Protecting Your ASC: A Legal Handbook**

(4) Diagnostic or therapeutic services or items directly related to the provision of a surgical procedure;

(5) Administrative, recordkeeping and housekeeping items and services; and

(6) Materials for anesthesia.

(7) Intra-ocular lenses (IOLs).

(8) Supervision of the services of an anesthetist by the operating surgeon.

(b) *Excluded services.* Facility services do not include items and services for which payment may be made under other provisions of part 405 of this chapter, such as physicians' services, laboratory, X-ray or diagnostic procedures (other than those directly related to performance of the surgical procedure), prosthetic devices (except IOLs), ambulance services, leg, arm, back and neck braces, artificial limbs, and durable medical equipment for use in the patient's home. In addition, they do not include anesthetist services furnished on or after January 1, 1989.

[56 FR 8844, Mar. 1, 1991, as amended at 57 FR 33899, July 31, 1992]

## Sec. 416.65  Covered surgical procedures.

Covered surgical procedures are those procedures that meet the standards described in paragraphs (a) and (b) of this section and are included in the list published in accordance with paragraph (c) of this section.

(a) *General standards.* Covered surgical procedures are those surgical and other medical procedures that—

(1) Are commonly performed on an inpatient basis in hospitals, but may be safely performed in an ASC;

(2) Are not of a type that are commonly performed, or that may be safely performed, in physicians' offices;

(3) Are limited to those requiring a dedicated operating room (or suite), and generally requiring a post-operative recovery room or short-term (not overnight) convalescent room; and

(4) Are not otherwise excluded under Sec. 405.310 of this chapter.

(b) *Specific standards.*

(1) Covered surgical procedures are limited to those that do not generally exceed—

(i) A total of 90 minutes operating time; and

(ii) A total of 4 hours recovery or convalescent time.

(2) If the covered surgical procedures require anesthesia, the anesthesia must be—

(i) Local or regional anesthesia; or

(ii) General anesthesia of 90 minutes or less duration.

(3) Covered surgical procedures may not be of a type that—

(i) Generally result in extensive blood loss;

(ii) Require major or prolonged invasion of body cavities;

(iii) Directly involve major blood vessels; or

(iv) Are generally emergency or life-threatening in nature.

(c) *Publication of covered procedures.* HCFA will publish in the Federal Register a list of covered surgical procedures and revisions as appropriate.

## Sec. 416.75 Performance of listed surgical procedures on an inpatient hospital basis.

The inclusion of any procedure as a covered surgical procedure under Sec. 416.65 does not preclude its coverage in an inpatient hospital setting under Medicare.

## Sec. 416.120 Basis for payment.

The basis for payment depends on where the services are furnished.

(a) *Hospital outpatient department.* Payment is in accordance with part 413 of this chapter.

(b) [Reserved]

(c) *ASC*—(1) *General rule.* Payment is based on a prospectively determined rate. This rate covers the cost of services such as supplies, nursing services, equipment, etc., as specified in Sec. 416.61. The rate does not cover physician services or other medical services covered under part 410 of this chapter (for example, X-ray services or laboratory services) which are not directly related to the performance of the surgical procedures. Those services may be billed separately and paid on a reasonable charge basis.

(2) *Single and multiple surgical procedures.* (i) If one covered surgical procedure is furnished to a beneficiary in an operative session, payment is based on the prospectively determined rate for that procedure.

**Protecting Your ASC: A Legal Handbook**

(ii) If more than one surgical procedure is furnished in a single operative session, payment is based on—

(A) The full rate for the procedure with the highest prospectively determined rate; and

(B) One half of the prospectively determined rate for each of the other procedures.

(3) *Deductibles and coinsurance.* Part B deductible and coinsurance amounts apply as specified in Sec. 410.152 (a) and (i) of this chapter.

[56 FR 8844, Mar. 1, 1991; 56 FR 23022, May 20, 1991]

## Sec. 416.125 ASC facility services payment rate.

(a) The payment rate is based on a prospectively determined standard overhead amount per procedure derived from an estimate of the costs incurred by ambulatory surgical centers generally in providing services furnished in connection with the performance of that procedure.

(b) The payment must be substantially less than would have been paid under the program if the procedure had been performed on an inpatient basis in a hospital.

[56 FR 8844, Mar. 1, 1991]

## Sec. 416.130 Publication of revised payment methodologies.

Whenever HCFA proposes to revise the payment rate for ASCs, HCFA publishes a notice in the Federal Register describing the revision. The notice also explains the basis on which the rates were established. After reviewing public comments, HCFA publishes a notice establishing the rates authorized by this section. In setting these rates, HCFA may adopt reasonable classifications of facilities and may establish different rates for different types of surgical procedures.

[47 FR 34094, Aug. 5, 1982, as amended at 56 FR 8844, Mar. 1, 1991]

# Sec. 416.140 Surveys.

(a) *Timing, purpose, and procedures.* (1) No more often than once a year, HCFA conducts a survey of a randomly selected sample of participating ASCs to collect data for analysis or reevaluation of payment rates.

(2) HCFA notifies the selected ASCs by mail of their selection and of the form and content of the report the ASCs are required to submit within 60 days of the notice.

(3) If the facility does not submit an adequate report in response to HCFA's survey request, HCFA may terminate the agreement to participate in the Medicare program as an ASC.

(4) HCFA may grant a 30-day postponement of the due date for the survey report if it determines that the facility has demonstrated good cause for the delay.

(b) *Requirements for ASCs.* ASCs must—

(1) Maintain adequate financial records, in the form and containing the data required by HCFA, to allow determination of the payment rates for covered surgical procedures furnished to Medicare beneficiaries under this subpart.

(2) Within 60 days of a request from HCFA submit, in the form and detail as may be required by HCFA, a report of—

(i) Their operations, including the allowable costs actually incurred for the period and the actual number and kinds of surgical procedures furnished during the period; and

(ii) Their customary charges for each surgical procedure furnished for the period.

[47 FR 34094, Aug. 5, 1982, as amended at 56 FR 8845, Mar. 1, 1991]

# Sec. 416.150 Beneficiary appeals.

A beneficiary (or ASC as his or her assignee) may request a hearing by a carrier (subject to the limitations and conditions set forth in part 405, subpart H of this chapter) if the beneficiary or the ASC—

(a) Is dissatisfied with a carrier's denial of a request for payment made on his or her behalf by an ASC;

(b) Is dissatisfied with the amount of payment; or

(c) Believes the request for payment is not being acted upon with reasonable promptness.

Protecting Your ASC: A Legal Handbook

# Endnotes

1. General Statutes of Connecticut Section 19a–637 (2001).

2. The copayment paid by Medicare beneficiaries for services in the hospital outpatient department may be larger for two reasons. First, the copayment for hospital services is based on the hospital charge for the service, with some limitations, whereas the ASC's payment is based on Medicare payments. Recently enacted legislation will gradually reduce the hospital copayment until it reaches 20% of Medicare payment as it does for ASC services. Even when the percentage is calculated on the same base, the copayments for hospital services will often be larger for the same service.

3. Mississippi State Department of Health and Q.S.C., LLC d/b/a First Choice Surgical Center v. Natchez Community Hospital

4. Gonzalez v. San Jacinto Methodist Hospital, 880 SW 2d, 436, 439 (Texas App 1999).

5. Mills v. Angel, 995 SW 2d, 262, 267 (Tx. Ct. App. 1999).

6. Texas Occupations Code Section 160.010 (2000).

7. St. Amant v. Thompson, 390 U.S. 727, 732, 88 S.Ct. 1323, 20 L.Ed.2d 262 (1968).

8. 26 C.F.R. §1.501 (c)(3)-1.

9. Redlands Surgical Services v. Commissioner, 113 T.C. 47(1999).

10. Redlands Surgical Services v. Commissioner, 9th Cir. No. 99-71253, (March 15, 2001).

11. United States v. Rockford Memorial Corp., 898 F.2d, 1278, 1282–83 (7th Cir. 1990) (quoting Hospital Corp. of America v. FTC, 807 F.2d, 1381, 1386 [7th Cir. 1986]).

12. United States v. Archer-Daniels-Midland Co., 866 F.2d 242, 246 (8th Cir. 1988), cert. denied, 493 U.S. 809, 110 S.Ct. 51, 107 L.Ed.2d 20 (1989).

13. HTI Health Services, Inc. Quorum Health Group, Inc. 960 F Supp 1104, 1127, & 1128 (SD Mississippi, Western Division 1997).

14. Hammond vs. Hospital Service District No. 1 of Tangipahoa Parish, 171 F.3d 231 (6th Cir. 1999).

15. OIG Advisory Opinion 98-12 (September 16, 1998), page 4.

16. *Ibid.*

17. *Ibid.*

18. 64 Federal Register No. 223 page 63536 (November 19, 1999).

19. 42 C.F.R. §1001.952(r)(1)(2000).

20. *Ibid.* at §1001.952(r)(2).

21. *Ibid.* at §1001.952(r)(3).

22. *Ibid.,* at §1001.952(r)(4).

23. 64 Federal Register No. 223 page 63537 (November 19, 1999).

24. 56 Federal Register 35952 (July 29, 1991).

25. *Ibid.*

26. *Ibid.*

27. 42 C.F.R. §424.73(b)(3)(ii).

28. HCFA Carriers Manual Part 3 (2265.2).

29. 64 Federal Register No.223 page 63536 (November 19, 1999).

30. 42 C.F.R. §416.43.

31. United States v. Krizek, 859 F. Supp. 5, 8 (D.D.C. 1994).

32. United States v. Lorenzo, 768 F. Supp. 1127 (E.D. Penn. 1991).

33. United States ex rel. Pogue v. American Healthcorp. Inc., 977 F. Supp. 1329 (M.D. Tenn. 1997).

34. United States ex rel. Joslin vs. Community Home Health of Maryland, Inc., 984 F. Supp. at 374, 376 (D. Maryland 1997).

35. Luckey v. Baxter Healthcare Corp., 2 F. Supp. 2d 1034, 1035 (N.D. Illinois 1998).

36. United States ex rel. Aranda, DeWitt v. Community Psychiatric Centers of Oklahoma, Inc., 945 F. Supp. 1485, 1488–89 (W.D. Okla. 1996).

**Protecting Your ASC: A Legal Handbook**

# Index

American Association for Accreditation of Ambulatory Surgery Facilities, Inc. (AAAASF) ............................12

Accreditation Association for Ambulatory Health Care (AAAHC) ............................12

Accreditation............12, 15, 36, 98

Americans with Disabilities Act (ADA) ............................37, 41

Adverse event ........................49–50

Advisory Opinions ............viii, 26, 78–79, 85–86

Anti-kickback issues....................vii, 26,65, 68, 77–79, 85–86, 88–89, 93

Antitrust ............vii, 35, 71–75, 79

Audits ....................24, 27–28, 87

Board of directors..................15–17

Bylaws................................31–36

C corporations......................57, 69

Certificate of Need (CON)....v, vii, 1–8, 62–64, 74, 93, 96

Civil Rights Act..........................39

Clayton Act....................71–73, 75

Clinical Laboratory Improvement Act (CLIA)..........................8–9

Centers for Medicare and Medicaid Services (CMS)....6, 12–13, 24, 78, 85–86, 103

CMS Form 1500..................24, 92

CMS Form 855....................13, 91

Consolidated Omnibus Budget Reconciliation Act of 1985 (COBRA)........................37, 43

Coding.............10–11, 23, 25, 27, 57–59, 91–92

Compensation ..39, 42, 55–56, 67, 83–88

Compliance plan ......vii, 19–29, 87

Consumer Credit Protection Act (CCPA) ..............................45

Controlled substances ................10

Copayment................6, 24, 78, 86

Current Procedural Terminology (CPT) codes..........................11

Credentialing..................31–36, 93

Drug Enforcement Administration (DEA) ............................10, 32

Deductible ........................24, 86, 99–100, 110

Deemed compliance ..................98

Deemed status....................12, 98

Discrimination..........19, 35, 39–42

Double billing....................21, 24

Downcoding ......................23, 92

Earnings before interest, taxes, depreciation and amortization (EBITDA) ............................64

Employee Polygraph Protection Act (EPPA) ..............................46

Equal Pay Amendment ..............38

Employee Retirement Income
Security Act (ERISA) ......42–43

Exemptions ..............................1–3

Fair Labor Standards Act
of 1938 ..............................37

Fair market value ................21, 26,
56–57, 64–68, 84, 87

False Claims Act (FCA) ............13,
19, 21, 23, 91–95

Family and Medical Leave Act
(FMLA) ...............................44

Fraud and abuse ....viii, 19–20, 23,
26, 28, 63, 85–86, 94

Garnishing Wages ................44–46

Governing body........15–17, 20, 27,
33, 36, 55–57, 102, 105–106

Hotline ..........................21, 27, 95

Immunity ......................34–35, 74

Inspector General ........viii, 26, 66,
78–79, 82–86

Immigration Reform and Control
Act of 1986 (IRCA) ..............41

Internal Revenue Service (IRS)..26,
51–55, 58, 65–66

Joint Commission on Accreditation
of Healthcare Organizations
(JCAHO) .......................... 12

Joint venture ......................vii, viii,
16, 51–59, 61–63, 71–72, 75

Kickbacks ..............19, 25, 77, 83

Labor union ........................44–45

Laboratory......................8–9, 22,
26, 83–84, 86, 107–109

Licensure...........viii, 1, 12, 62–63,
77, 93–94, 98, 102

Lie detector ..........................46–47

Medicaid .............vii–viii, 6, 9, 26,
32, 40, 77–78, 84, 88, 95

Medical devices ....................49, 50

Medicare ............v, vii–viii, 1, 3, 6,
9–15, 21, 23–26, 31–33, 36,
40, 43, 63, 77–78, 80–81,
84–86, 88, 91–94, 97, 99–102,
107, 109, 111

Medicare certification.................1,
11–14, 93

Minutes..............7–8, 16, 108–109

Monopoly ..........................71–73

National Labor Rights
Act (NLRA) ..........................44

Notice ..............13, 15, 25, 37–38,
43–45, 98–101, 110–111

National Practitioner Data Bank
(NPDB) ...............................32

Occupational Safety and Health Act
(OSHA) ...............................42

Pension .............39, 42, 51, 58–59

Pharmacy license ......................10

Provider-performed microscopy
(PPMP) certificate ................. 9

Price fixing..........................71–74

**Protecting Your ASC: A Legal Handbook**          **115**

Privileging ............................31–36

Quality assurance ......................54

*Qui tam*...........................91, 93, 94

Redlands Surgical Services....53–54

Referrals ...............viii, 19, 25–27, 66–89, 107

Rehabilitation Act of 1973 ..39, 40

Safe harbors ........................vii, 68, 79–83, 84–86

Safe Medical Devices Act of 1990............................49–50

Self-referral...........................viii, 77

Sherman Act .......................71–75

Stark law ..........viii, 26, 77, 88–89

Tax shelter............................57–58

Taxes ..........45–46, 51, 53, 57–59, 63–64, 68–69

Uniformed Services Employment and Reemployment Rights Act (USERRA)......................38

Upcoding..............................23, 92

Valuation..................56, 63–65, 87

Veterans.....................................41

Vietnam Era Veterans' Readjustment Act of 1974 ....41

Wages ......................37–38, 45–47

Wagner Act of 1935..............44–45